REVELATION

THE BRIDGE BIBLE TRANSLATION

Connecting the Biblical to the Contemporary World

CONTENTS

REVELATION

—

1. Introduction: Christ reveals God's divine mysteries (section spanning Chapter 1:1—1:20).

CHAPTER 1

1.1 Christ unveils the picture of God's plan and provides the purpose of Revelation (1:1-3).

[1]This letter reveals God's divine mysteries. It comes from Jesus Christ. God gave Him this revelation to give to us, His servants, that we may understand the events that are happening now and others that must soon take place. This unveiled picture of God's revelation and plans comes to us through a five-step process. First, the revelation began with God's plan. Second, it was received by Jesus. Third, Jesus shared it with an angel. Fourth, the angel was tasked to share it with John. [2]Fifth, John faithfully reported everything he saw from the angel as a reliable witness.

This letter is John's report on that revelation, and it provides two things: 1) a clear message from God and 2) a written statement and official account of the truth found in Jesus Christ. [3]Since this letter of revelation comes directly from God, those who read it aloud will have a divine sense of fulfillment. Moreover, those who hear it and live by what is written will have a divine sense of fulfillment flowing through their lives. Why? Because God's kingdom has come, and these things are happening now.

1.2 Christ unveils the picture of God's plan, which shows He is in control of history and all things—everything that is, has been, and will be (1:4-8).

⁴I, John, am writing this letter.

I am writing it to the churches in the province of Asia.

May you live in God's unmerited favor and experience His peace. These qualities come from the one God who eternally exists in three persons:

1) from the Father, who is the focal point of everything that is, was, or will be (the present, past, and future);
2) from the Holy Spirit, who indwells believers, connects the church, and lives before God's throne; ⁵and
3) from Jesus Christ, who is:
   a. the Prophet faithfully witnessing about the way of salvation,
   b. the Priest who demonstrated He made an acceptable sacrifice for sin by rising from the dead, and
   c. the King who is above any earthly rulers.

What an amazing God we have! All worth and all power belong to Jesus Christ! Why? Because He is the One who loves us, and because He freed us from all our sins through His blood. Like the Passover lamb in Exodus, by His one blood sacrifice, we are freed from sin.

⁶Through His sacrifice, Christ broke us out of sin's prison and brought us into His kingdom. He changed our position from being slaves to sin to being a community of co-rulers, agents, and messengers who serve God the Father. As a result, forever, He will be our greatest worth! Forever, His power will rule! We know these things to be true—that Christ is coming and is already on His way!

⁷His arrival will be an amazing sight to behold! He will come riding through the clouds, just as prophesied by Daniel 7:13-14. When He appears, no one will miss it. Every eye will see Him. Everyone who

mocked Him and played a part in His death will see Christ for who
He truly is. Upon realizing who He is and how they played a part
in His death, all the people on earth will mourn over what they did
to Him just as Zechariah 12:10 predicted. It will be a terribly amazing and gloriously humbling arrival! And we know these things to be
true—that Christ is coming and that He is on His way!

⁸Remember what the Lord God says: "I am the beginning and the
end of all things. My sovereign power and divine will are in control of
history—everything that is, was, and will be."

1.3 Christ unveils the picture of God's plan, which shows that God's Church is secure in His hand (1:9-20).

⁹I, John, am your partner in suffering, and I am writing to you from
the Roman island prison of Patmos. I have been banished here because
of my public sharing of God's message and because of my public statement—my official account—of the truth found in Jesus Christ. I am
your fellow companion living for Christ's kingdom, experiencing suffering, and learning to endure patiently in this world as we live in
Jesus Christ.

¹⁰On Sunday, the first day of the week set aside to celebrate and
honor the Lord Jesus, I was spiritually focused and filled with the
Holy Spirit. Through the Spirit's special movement on this unique,
one-time, revelatory occasion, I was transported to a spiritual place, a
spiritual realm, where God could reveal these prophetic visions to me.
In this spiritual realm, I heard a loud, trumpet-like voice—which also
had peaceful and guiding qualities—behind me.

¹¹The voice said, "Write down everything you see and send it to the
seven churches in Ephesus, Smyrna, Pergamum, Thyatira, Sardis,
Philadelphia, and Laodicea. These seven churches are in key strategic
and distributive centers. By sharing this letter with them, these visions
will be able to reach the world."

¹²I turned to see the voice that was speaking to me. What I saw was the

most profound thing one could ever see! Before I describe what I saw, let me first tell you the main point of all these amazing descriptions I am about to share with you. The main point is this: that the One I saw had all the glory of heaven and all the fullness of God. He is the One who fulfilled all the Old Covenant's [Old Testament's] prophecies about the Messiah, the Anointed One who decisively delivers God's people. Keep this main point in mind as I try to describe what I saw with the most vivid word pictures I am capable of.

I saw seven golden lampstands in this heavenly spiritual realm. These seven golden lampstands represent the universal Church, all of God's people. [13]Among the seven golden lampstands, I saw the One who the prophet Daniel wrote about in Daniel 7:13. Daniel wrote that "someone like the son of man" would come. He would be a fully divine, yet fully human person. He would be full of God's glory and be the One to bring God's kingdom deliverance to all. The One Daniel was referring to is who I saw!

He was dressed in a robe that stretched down to His feet and had a golden sash across His chest. The robe and golden sash were priestly garments that indicated this One is more important and has more authority than any previous Old Covenant [Old Testament] priest.

[14]His hair was white like wool, whiter than the whitest snow. The whiteness of His hair symbolizes that God has all the wisdom of a wise ruler and judge, that He is worthy of ultimate respect. Just as Daniel mentioned about the "son of man' in Daniel 10:6, His eyes were like blazing fire, which symbolizes His holy yet fierce judgment.

[15]His feet were like bright bronze that had been purified in a furnace. From the prophetic times during the Old Covenant [Old Testament], this bright bronze symbolizes victory—more specifically, the victory of the One who had delivered a triumphant judgment over the unfaithful. His voice sounded like the most powerful, mightiest waterfall a person could ever hear, which symbolizes His awe-inspiring power and majesty.

[16]In His right hand, He held seven stars. The seven stars symbolize how God holds the universal Church in His hand. I am so accustomed to seeing churches separated geographically and Christians being divided for one reason or another, and it may occasionally look that way on earth. But in the heavenly spiritual realm, I saw that God holds the church in His right hand—the hand which was associated with power and safety. In this instance, He was holding the universal Church safely in His power. I also saw a sharp, double-edged sword coming out of His mouth. It symbolizes how God's just truth pierces the heart and is victorious over all other truth claims. And the light shining from His face was so brilliant, so bright that it was overwhelming. It reminded me of God's overwhelming glory and worth.

[17]When I saw Him and His all-surpassing worth, I fell at His feet. How could I do anything else? I was standing in front of the Eternal One! I was so fearful. I thought I would die for sure, but then He spoke to me.

He said: "Do not be afraid of me. I am the First and the Last—the Lord of history and the Creator of all things. [18]I am the One who has life, who gives life, and who is life. Even though they put Me to death, it did not stop the Divine-life in Me. The Divine, resurrecting power of God gave new life to My resurrected body, and this new life shall never be extinguished. By taking on human form, dying a physical death that paid the price for sin, and rising from the dead, I have unlocked the door to heaven. Having unlocked the door, I hold the keys to the Divine-life that is beyond death for everyone.

[19]"Now, write down every part of this vision—what you have seen, what you are seeing, and what you will see later. [20]But before we talk about the circumstances troubling the universal Church, did you understand both the imagery of the seven stars I hold in My right hand and the seven golden lampstands? They are essential for what I am about to tell you. Let us review and make sure you understood them.

"The seven stars symbolize the spiritual, heavenly beings—the spiritual messengers—who watch over each of the seven churches I am about to mention to you. (And yes, each church has a heavenly being who works for it in the heavenly spiritual realm). The seven lampstands symbolize the seven churches on earth we are about to discuss.

"What is the overall meaning that you need to keep in mind in this vision? That the universal Church is secure. I hold the Church—the universal collective of all my followers—in My hand. I watch over the Church. As a result, I have some things to say to it. I am going to address each church individually to highlight a particular issue in it. However, this letter will be circulated among all churches. What I say about one church applies to them all."

2. Seven messages, one theme: Even though suffering will exist in this world, God encourages His people, His universal Church, to remain faithful (section spanning Chapter 2:1–3:22).

CHAPTER 2

2.1 Message one through the church at Ephesus: Remain faithful in your love for God (2:1-7).

[1]"Write the following to the heavenly messenger looking over the church in Ephesus—the church that is at the crossroads of the world—and to all the people in it:

'I am the One who holds the Church—represented by the seven stars—in My right hand. I walk in the midst of the Church, which is symbolized by the seven golden lampstands. In an unsure world, I secure and ensure the Church's existence. These are My words to you.

[2]'I know the good things you do—your hard work, your troubles, and the hardships you have patiently endured while serving Me. I know you cannot tolerate those who do evil and that you are especially good at discovering false apostles. They claim to be special messengers

from God who bring divine truth, but you see through their lies. You know they are imposters and are good at staying true to your doctrinal beliefs. [3]I know you show great perseverance and have endured hardship in living a Christian life. Courageously, you have not grown weary of serving Me.

[4]"Even though I know these things, I am holding something significant against you: You have forsaken and left your first love. [5]Do you not remember how strong your love for Me [Christ] and one another used to be? Ponder how far you have fallen and repent! Turn back to God and live like you used to—with a life filled with love. If you do not repent, you are on a dangerous path. If you do not turn back to God, I will come to you in judgment and will not recognize you as one of My churches any longer. Symbolically, your lampstand will be snuffed out and removed from its place in My presence. [6]Yes, you have a hatred for the false teaching and practices of those in the Nicolaitan sect, which I also hate. But do not get so caught up in doctrinal battles with them that you lose your love for Me or others.

[7]"Whoever has ears should use them to listen to what I am saying through the Holy Spirit to the Church. To the ones who overcome and live in faithful love, I will give the tree of life. The tree of life symbolically represents how you will have eternal life and dwell in God's presence. For the one who has the tree of life, it will be like returning to the Garden of Eden. There, you will live with God forever in perfect peace.'"

2.2 Message two through the church in Smyrna: Remain faithful no matter what may come (or till the end) (2:8-11).

[8]"Write the following to the heavenly messenger and people at the church in the prosperous seaport city of Smyrna. These words come from the One who is the beginning and end of all things, the One who died to pay the price for sin and came back to life again, winning a decisive victory over death:

⁹"I know the persecution you have endured because of Me. Even though you are in a city of great wealth, I know you have experienced poverty. Yet, through it all, you have felt extremely rich because of your life with Me. I know there are people pretending to be good Jews who are slandering you. But regardless of their pretense, they are acting as agents of Satan.

¹⁰"Even though you face persecution, do not be afraid of the sufferings you are about to endure. The Devil and his agents will put some of you in prison to test you and your faith. There, you will experience additional suffering for a short period of time. But do not give in to their injustice and imprisonment. Be faithful throughout it. Even if they pass a death sentence on you, be faithful. If you remain faithful, I will be excited to give you the victory crown of eternal life with Me.

¹¹"Whoever has ears should use them to listen to what I am saying through the Holy Spirit to the Church. Even though you may experience pain, suffering, or death in this life, be faithful. The one who is victorious and remains faithful to the end will not experience the dreadful second death—the spiritual and eternal death reserved for those who will be forever separated from God when He passes His final judgment.'"

2.3 Message three through the church in Pergamum: Remain faithful against false religious teachings (2:12-17).

¹²"Write the following to the heavenly messenger and people of the church at Pergamum:

'I am the One who speaks the truth like a sharp, double-edged sword. The truth I speak cuts to the very heart of the matter, and these are My words to you.

¹³"I know what life is like in Pergamum. You live in a city that is a religious center for idolatry and the worship of pagan gods. The quasi-religious idolatry of emperor worship surrounds you. False worship of false things is so strong in Pergamum that it seems like Satan has

his throne there. Yet, in the midst of such strong religious opposition, you have remained faithful to Me. Even though you have encountered hostility, you did not give up or turn away from your faith. You did not renounce Me even when facing death, like Antipas—a faithful witness—who was killed for not renouncing his faith. What a foothold Satan has on this city! It is like he lives in Pergamum and makes it his home.

[14]"Even though you remain faithful in the face of opposition, I regret to say I have a few things against you. You are prone to follow false teaching. Some follow the truth faithfully, like Antipas. But others among you follow other religious teachings. You are trying to hold on to My truth and these other false religious teachings at the same time—as though they are equal.

'The first false teaching that has infiltrated your community is the untrue teaching of Balaam. In the Scriptures of the Old Covenant [Old Testament], the false teacher Balaam taught Balak to entice the Israelites to eat food sacrificed to idols. He also falsely taught them to engage in sexually immoral acts with temple prostitutes as an act of worship to false deities. Just as Balak and the Israelites gave in to Balaam's false teaching, some people among you have fallen prey to these same deceptive, immoral, and false religious practices.

[15]"The second false teaching that has infiltrated your community is the untrue teaching of the Nicolaitans. This false teaching proposes a radical division between body and spirit—that the body is all evil and only the spirit is good. As such, it expresses that people can do immoral things because they are of the body while maintaining they are morally and spiritually free because their spirit is good. This false teaching develops a wrong sense of religious freedom and perpetuates immoral actions. Some people in your church are falling prey to this false teaching.

[16]"Not recognizing either of these false teachings is extremely dangerous! You need to repent and turn fully back to God! Otherwise, I will soon come to you and will wield My truth like a mighty sword in order to destroy those following these false teachings.

[17]'Whoever has ears should use them to listen to what I am saying through the Holy Spirit to the Church. To the one who overcomes false religion and is victorious through faith, I will give fulfilling spiritual nourishment, which will surpass any of the big banquets to pagan gods going on around you. I will also give you a membership card into My family and My kingdom. As an accepted member, you will know and experience things that are divinely unique and beyond this world—things that surpass mere mortal existence and will be shared by none except those who belong to My family.'"

2.4 Message four through the church in Thyatira: Remain faithful by avoiding immoral practices and enduring opposition in the world (2:18-29).

[18]"Write the following to the heavenly messenger and people of the church at Thyatira:

'I, Jesus, am the Son of God. The Roman emperor may like to be called by that title and falsely worshipped as such. But I am the true Son of God—the One who ultimately provides salvation to God's people. As the Son of God, I have eyes that blaze brighter than the sun. The so-called Roman sun deity does even not come close to My greatness. My feet have been refined by blazing furnace fires, and they shine like bronze. My blazing eyes and fire-refined feet let you know I have a consuming passion for justice and the strength to make right judgments. There is no comparison between how great My justice and strength are and that of anyone else. Earthly rulers and false deities do not even come close.

[19]'I know of the good things you have done. I have deep knowledge of your strong love and faith. I also know of your dedicated service and faithful perseverance, and that your church has grown consistently.

[20]'Even though I know these things, I have something serious against you. You are allowing yourselves to be led astray by that false woman who calls herself a prophet. She is leading those who serve Me astray

like a modern-day Jezebel, leading you toward idolatry and away from God. This so-called false prophetess teaches you to:

1) indulge in immoral sexual practices and to abuse your freedom in Christ,
2) falsely and intentionally leads you to break religious customs, and
3) fools you into thinking you are somehow living on a higher level of morality than others.

²¹I have called this Jezebel-like prophetess to repentance and given her time to respond. But she is unwilling to turn back to Me.

²²'As a result, I will throw her onto a bed of anguish and suffering. I will make those who commit adultery with her suffer intense pain. Unless they repent of following her false ways and return to Me, suffering awaits them. ²³I will strike her children dead. Then all the churches will know I am the One who searches everyone's hearts and that I have access to the totality of their minds. And as I search hearts and minds, I will repay each of you according to what you have done.

²⁴'Now to the rest of you in Thyatira, I will not impose a burden on you. By "the rest of you," I am referring to two groups: 1) the faithful ones who do not hold to the false teachings of that Jezebel-like woman and 2) to the ones who have not been suckered by those false apostles into believing the so-called "special revelations into Satan's deep secrets." To you faithful ones in Thyatira, you will not experience any burden.

²⁵'Instead, I want to encourage you. I encourage you to continue to hold onto God's teachings until I come again and reveal all things to you. ²⁶To everyone who overcomes these temptations and remains victorious, to all who do My will throughout their life, I will give them the authority to rule over the nations with Me.

²⁷'Right now, in this world, you may be ruled over by others. But for those who are faithful to the end, you will rule over all the faithless and powers of the world with Me. With the authority I give you, you

will have the power to break through hearts. You will be able to break through them as easily as an iron scepter can smash clay pots into many broken pieces. Just as My Father gave Me full authority to rule over all things, I will share it with you.

²⁸"This is similar to how the Romans behave when they are victorious. They like to give credit to the false goddess Venus. They call Venus their morning star, and they use the star as a symbol of Venus's victory and sovereign rule over others. The difference: I will not give you a fake symbol but the true Morning Star—the eternal symbol of victory from the one Sovereign ruler over all things. You will have Me, and you can rest assured that you will triumph and rule with Me.

²⁹"Whoever has ears should use them to listen to what I am saying through the Holy Spirit to the Church.'"

CHAPTER 3

2.5 Message five through the church in Sardis: Remain faithful by maintaining a healthy, inward spiritual life (3:1-6).

¹"Write the following to the heavenly messenger and people of the church at Sardis:

'I am the One who holds both the life-giving Spirit of God (symbolized by the seven spirits) and the whole Church (symbolized by the seven stars) in My hand. These are My words to you.

'I know you have a reputation for doing good things and for being vibrantly alive. But you are spiritually dead. Your outward appearance and reputation for being alive is just a show. There is no real spiritual life in you.

²"This is your wakeup call! You need to pay attention! Even though your reputation looks good on the outside, I know the reality. I know the things you do are just the smoke and mirrors that hide your real spiritual unhealthiness and complacency. In reality, your spiritual pulse is weak. Worse, your spiritual pulse is fading and approaching

a flatline. You will die if you do not begin spiritually exercising and strengthening yourself again.

³'Do you not remember how you reacted when you first received and heard God's truth? Your initial positive response to the gospel is well known. But you have lost it! You need to remember what it was like when real life flowed through you. You need to turn back to God and hold on tightly to your faith in Him. If you do not wake up, if you do not respond to these spiritual health warnings, I will bring judgment upon you. Sadly, you will not even see it coming. You will be like the people from your city in the past who thought their fortified city walls could not be taken over. Yet, in stealth mode, others crept in and destroyed them. In a similar fashion, you will not see it coming. My judgment will sneak up on you like a thief who takes everything you have without you even knowing he was there.

⁴'But all hope is not lost! There are a few people in Sardis whose faith and godly living are apparent. They stick out like a spotless, bright white shirt among the rags of filthy clothes. These faithful people are worthy of walking with Me no matter what happens to you. ⁵For those among you who are victorious in turning back and following Me, your belief and godly living will be evident as faithful ones. Your faithfulness will also be as apparent as a spotless, bright white shirt among a bunch of filthy rags. But more importantly, those who turn back to follow Me will never have to worry about Me blotting out their name from the book of life. Every person's name recorded in the book of life belongs to God's family. And I will let My Father and the angels know that your name is there, that you belong to Our family.

⁶'Whoever has ears should use them to listen to what I am saying through the Spirit to the Church.'"

2.6 Message six through the church in Philadelphia: Remain faithful knowing that God provides safety and makes an eternal, positive example of the faithful (3:7-13).

⁷"Write the following to the heavenly messenger and people of the church at Philadelphia:

'I, Jesus, am the One who was promised to come, the Messiah who will deliver God's people. Let Me remind you of a few of My attributes.

1. I am the holy One—the God who is set apart and unlike anything else in the universe. I am not just another person; I am the holy God.
2. I am the true One who is wholly trustworthy.
3. I am the One who holds the key of David—meaning, I decide who gets into God's kingdom and who does not. Whenever I open the door to let someone in, no one can shut it to keep that person out. Whenever I close the door on someone to keep them out, no one can open it to let that person in. These are My words to you.

⁸'I know the reality about you. I have opened the door to God's kingdom for those who love Me, and you are leading others to that door. Even though you are a small congregation with little societal influence in a large, culturally influential city, you are not only opening the door to others but have faced intense persecution in doing so. During these times, you have remained strong. You have stayed true to My teachings. You have not denied being My followers.

⁹'As for those unbelieving, false Jewish teachers who like to persecute you, I will make them come and bow down at your feet. They claim to belong to God via Jewish heritage, but they do not. These false teachers belong to the synagogue of Satan, not Me. Though this false religious group is strong now, I will make them bow before you. In shame and humility, they will see the truth as it is and will have to acknowledge that I have indeed loved you as My people, not them.

¹⁰'Since you have kept My command to endure suffering patiently, I will keep you safe from the hour of trial and testing that is going to come upon the entire world. That time of trial will test all those who live on the earth, but you will be protected and safe from it. ¹¹I am coming soon to bring about that time. Until then, continue to remain

strong. Hold on to the truth you have in Me so that no one can steal your victor's crown away from you.

¹²'Where you are in Philadelphia, you are accustomed to earthquakes. For those who overcome and are victorious in the faith, I will make you strong pillars in the temple of God's kingdom. They will be secure and immovable; nothing will be able to shake them. And they will not just be ordinary pillars. They will be pillars that have My name permanently inscribed upon them. In Philadelphia's history, your city has undergone various rulers, governments, and name changes. But God's kingdom is permanent, and so is your place there. God's rule will never end. And the name of God's city—the new, heavenly Jerusalem, which will break into human existence from heaven after the final judgment—will not change. Its name will be permanent. Even though you may have little influence and strength now, you will be an eternal pillar in God's kingdom that has My name permanently written on you, making it clear that you belong there forever.

¹³'Whoever has ears should use them to listen to what I am saying through the Holy Spirit to the Church.'"

2.7 Message seven through the church in Laodicea: Remain faithful by recognizing what true wealth is, where it comes from, and responding to the One who gives it (3:14-22).

¹⁴"Write the following to the heavenly messenger and people of the church at Laodicea:

'I, Jesus, am the Amen—the strong affirmation of God in this world. I am the One who embodies faithfulness and provides an accurate and true account of all things. I am the One who guarantees and executes God's purposes, the primary source of all creation. These are My words to you.

¹⁵'I know the reality about you. The best water around Laodicea is actively moving, whether the hot spring in Hierapolis or the cold stream in Colosse. But unlike these good waters, your life toward Me

is neither hot nor cold. I wish you were one or the other; then, you would be active and useful. [16]Instead, you are lukewarm—neither hot nor cold. You are like the stagnant waters off the Lycus River; they are known for their impurity and for making people sick. If you were water and I took a drink of you, I would instantly spit your filthiness out of My mouth.

[17]"Because you are in a commercial center known for its wealth, you like to say, "I am rich; I have achieved great wealth and do not need a thing." Sadly, you do not recognize just how wretched, pitiful, poor, blind, and naked you really are! [18]Even though you are surrounded by financial wealth, I counsel you to trust in and invest in the gold I offer—gold that has been purified and refined by fire. By investing in My gold, you will become genuinely rich. Even though you are surrounded by clothing manufacturers, I counsel you to trust in and purchase the heavenly clothing I offer—garments of moral perfection. By buying and wearing My clothes, your guilt and shame will be covered. Even though you have good physicians, I counsel you to trust in the treatment I offer for your eye condition. By using My eye treatment, your blindness will be healed, and you will be able to see.

[19]"Do not be surprised by My words. I love you enough to rebuke and correct you when needed. If I did not love you and want the best for you, I would not bother. But here is your chance! Be enthusiastic in responding to My correction and follow Me.

[20]"I am here now, right in front of you! I am standing at the front door knocking. If anyone hears Me, responds, and opens the door, I will come in. We will have a solid relationship. I will be with them throughout life, even in the most common elements of daily living. [21]For those who are victorious in their faith, I will give a place of authority and rule in the world to come. Just as I was victorious over sin, death, and the Devil, and just as My Father gave Me a place of authority and rule, I will do the same for you. Those who are victorious through faith will share in Our authority and rule in God's kingdom.

[22]"Whoever has ears should use them to listen to what I am saying through the Holy Spirit to the Church.'"

3. The big picture: Even though suffering will exist in this
    world, God has a bigger plan beyond what we can see
    (section spanning Chapter 4:1–5:14).

CHAPTER 4

3.1 God provides a glimpse inside heaven (4:1-11).

3.1.1   Heaven is a place where God rules (4:1-2).

¹After I had heard Jesus' message to the Church through these seven
churches, I was astonished to see a door standing open. It was a door
that took me into the spiritual realm that exists in the air all around
us. And it was not just any door. It was a door into the main headquarters of heaven, where all plans are made. As I stood looking at
the door, the same powerful, trumpet-like voice spoke to me again,
saying, "Come and join Me in the main headquarters—Our control
room. I will show you God's big-picture plan for history from this
moment forward."

²Accepting the invitation to enter through the door, my eyes became
fully open. I saw into heaven, the spiritual realm that exists in the air
around us. I was inside heaven's main headquarters. And what caught
my attention and overwhelmed me most out of everything I was seeing? The glorious throne of the eternal God and the One seated on
it! Words can never fully convey the amazement of what I saw, nor
the power and richness of it. It was humbling and overwhelming!
Realizing that my words will never convey how terrifically amazing
the sight really is, I will do my best to describe what I saw to you.

*3.1.2   Heaven is a place centered on God's greatness and filled
         will His glory (4:3-7).*

³The One seated on the throne appeared in a crystalline brightness,
like the sharpest, purest diamond. He appeared in a fiery fullness
brighter than the greatest of red rubies. The powerful visuals of what I
saw made clear the majestic splendor of the One seated on the throne.
The scene clearly communicated that the One on the throne was the

Supreme King and spiritual ruler of the universe. The glorious throne was encircled by an amazing, majestic rainbow that shone like a bright emerald. The emerald-like rainbow's appearance reminded me of the symbolism of the rainbow that appeared after Noah's ark in the book of Genesis. After that great flood, God used the symbol of a rainbow to remind Noah and humanity of His great mercy toward them.

⁴Surrounding the central location of the glorious throne were twenty-four other thrones. These twenty-four other thrones were in a circular pattern around the glorious throne. Seated on each of these thrones were the twelve tribes of Israel from the Scriptures of the Old Covenant [Old Testament] and the twelve apostles of the God's New Covenant through Christ [New Testament]. These twenty-four leaders were seated on the twenty-four thrones because they—chosen and appointed by God—communicated His foundational teachings to the world. The twenty-four leaders were dressed in white and had gold crowns on their heads. They looked like great, victorious athletes who had finished running their race well.

⁵Out from the glorious central throne came flashes of lightning and thunderous reverberations. Their power reminded me of when God spoke to Moses on Mount Sinai in Exodus 19. In front of the glorious throne was a blazing, seven-branched lampstand, which symbolized the presence of the Holy Spirit. This blazing, seven-branched lampstand also reminded me of the one used in the temple of Jerusalem. Just like the symbolic meaning of that lampstand, this one made me think about how God's full and complete presence is with us via the Person of the Holy Spirit.

⁶Also, in front of the central throne was the purest sea I have ever seen. It was so crystal clear that it looked like a sheet of glass. Its meaning was not lost on me, as it symbolized how crystal clear and pure everyone must be before approaching God, and that we gain this crystal-clear purity through Christ.

⁷Centrally positioned around the glorious throne in four main directions—north, south, east, and west—were four living creatures. They represented the created world where God's power and rule are always

active. These four living creatures were covered with eyes in front and in back. Their eyes in front and back reminded me of how God has all vision and knowledge; His vision spans time in all directions— vision and knowledge of both what is future and what is past. The first living creature was like a lion; it made me think of God's majesty and supreme rule over the created world. The second living creature was like an ox; it reminded me of God's strength, power, labor, and patience over creation. The third living creature had a face like a human being; it implied to me God's reason, intelligence, and emotion over the created world. The fourth living creature was like a flying eagle; it reminded me of God's loftiness and His presence that is above all in creation.

3.1.3 Heaven is a place where God's creation and God's people worship Him (4:8-11).

[8]Each of these four living creatures, which symbolize nature and God's creation, had six wings. Their six wings represent God's ability to look over His created world without stopping or growing weary. These four living creatures also had eyes covering their bodies in all directions. They symbolized God's ceaseless ability to watch over all aspects of His creation. Day and night, these four living creatures never tire. They never desire to stop worshipping God. They give glory to God by saying:

> "Holy, holy, holy
> Is the Creator of the universe, the Almighty God over all things.
> He is the eternal One who always was, Who presently is, and
> who is to come."

[9]And then something amazing happened! Whenever these four living creatures, who represent God's created world, worshiped the One who sits on the throne, [10]the twenty-four leaders, representing God's people, also joined in. Next, the twenty-four leaders bowed down before the One who sits on the throne. They worshiped the Eternal One who lives forever. Then the twenty-four leaders took off their crowns of victorious, faithful living and laid them down before the Eternal One's glorious throne. They said:

¹¹"You alone are worthy of all our praise,
>   You are the Just Ruler over all of us. You are the
>   Being of which there is none higher.
>   You alone are more valuable than anything else
>   in the universe. You alone are worthy of
>   receiving all our greatest thoughts and all
>   our greatest energies,
>   For You are the Creator who made all things.
>   By Your will and desire, all things were created
>   and have their being."

The scene around the throne is beyond comprehension. My meager description does not do it justice! It is overwhelming, indescribable! God's creation (represented by the four living creatures) and the twenty-four leaders (representing God's people) join together in the universal praise and worship of the One who alone is worthy of receiving it. It was a magnificent scene, but it was also a place I felt I had been created to live in. It was like my whole life's purpose and journey was to be right there forever!

CHAPTER 5

3.2 Christ alone can reveal God's plan (5:1-14).

3.2.1 Who can unveil God's plan for human history? (5:1-2)

¹As this chorus of universal praise—from those representing both God's creation and God's people—continued, I then saw a scroll in the right hand of the One who sat on the throne. Like an ancient, legally significant contract, the scroll had writing on both sides, and it was sealed with seven seals. These seven seals implied that a scroll was completely sealed off from being opened until the appropriate and appointed time. The scroll in His hand was extremely special. It contained God's unveiled narrative and plan for history, including how He will fulfill His covenant promise for all things.

²As I was looking at the scroll, I heard a mighty angel. His voice was powerful enough to echo through the entire heavens. He asked a perplexing question: "Who is worthy to break these seals, to open up the scroll of God's plan for history, and explain it to us?"

3.2.2 No one is worthy to unveil God's plan (5:3-4).

³There was complete silence as the angel's question lingered throughout heaven. The realization struck us all that no one in the spiritual realm of heaven, no one in the skies above the earth, no one on the earth, nor anyone in the realm of the dead could open the scroll. No one in any realm of existence was worthy to take a glimpse into the scroll of God's plan.

⁴As the angel's question hung in the air of heaven, we all felt an overwhelming sadness. No one was worthy to open the scroll of God's plan for history and explain it to us! I wept with deep sadness because no one could even peek into the smallest portion of it.

3.2.3 Christ is worthy and will unveil God's plan for history (5:5).

⁵Yet, while sorrow and sadness filled my entire being, one of the twenty-four leaders came to me and said, "You do not have to weep. There is good news! Look at the powerful and majestic Lion God raised up from the tribe of Judah! This Lion is the promised root (or offspring) that Daniel prophesied would come to deliver God's people. Because of who He is and what He has done, He alone is able to open the scroll of God's plan for history. He can break each of the seven seals."

3.2.4 Christ is worthy because of His crucifixion and resurrection (5:6-8).

⁶Then I saw a pure Lamb who had the marks of sacrificial slaughter on His body—similar to the Passover lamb mentioned in Exodus. This sacrificed Lamb was standing at the center of the throne fully alive and fully victorious over death! This sacrificed, resurrected Lamb at the center of the throne was encircled by the four living creatures (representing God's created world) and the twenty-four leaders

(representing God's people). The sacrificed, resurrected Lamb had seven horns, which reminded me of God's complete power, authority, and rule over all things. The sacrificed, resurrected Lamb also had seven eyes, which made me think of how God's Spirit sees everything and is actively moving over all the earth all the time.

[7]The sacrificed-yet-living Lamb approached the glorious throne. He was allowed to take the scroll of God's plan from the right hand of Him who sat on the throne. [8]When the Lamb had taken the scroll, the four living creatures (representing God's creation) and the twenty-four leaders (representing God's people) bowed down before the Lamb in worship. Each one held instruments to assist in worship—a harp to make music with and a golden bowl filled with incense, which represented the prayers of God's people.

3.2.5 All creation and all God's people celebrate Christ's worth and God's plan (5:9-14).

[9]Together, they sang a new song—a song that highlighted the Messiah's gift of life and the new era of life He brings about. They sang:

> "You alone have all value and worth. You alone are worthy
>   of holding the scroll of God's plan for history in your hands.
>   You alone are capable of opening its seals.
> You alone are worthy because You were sacrificially slain on
>   humanity's behalf. You alone are worthy because Your
>   blood purchased for God a redeemed people from every
>   tribe, language, people group, and nation in the world.
> [10]You have made Your redeemed people into a kingdom—
>   an active community that fully lives as You would have
>   them to.
> You have also made them all individual priests who serve God
>   through their lives and actions. Your redeemed community
>   of priestly kings will reign on the earth."

[11]Just when I thought I had seen all my senses could handle, I looked again and was shocked beyond belief. I heard the largest chorus imaginable—produced by thousands upon thousands of angels—singing

in perfect unison. There were so many angels singing that I could not comprehend how many there were. This great multitude of angels, along with the four living creatures (representing God's creation) and the twenty-four leaders (representing God's redeemed people), encircled the glorious throne at the center.

[12]They sang in a loud, unified voice:

> "You alone have all value and are worthy. As the sacrificial Lamb
>   who brings and gives life to all,
> You alone are worthy to receive all power, wealth, wisdom,
>   strength, honor, glory, and praise!"

[13]As though that was not a big enough choir to convey the glory of the Lamb, I then heard every creature in the sky, on the earth, under the earth, and in the sea—all living things—join together in worship, saying:

> "To the One who sits on the throne and to the sacrificial Lamb
>   who gives us life,
> You are our highest approval, thought, value, worth, and
>   strength that can be known, both now and forever!"

[14]The four living creatures (representing God's creation) said, "Amen, it will always be so," and the twenty-four leaders (representing God's people) fell down to their knees and joined in the universal chorus worshipping God.

4. The seven seals: Even though suffering will exist in this world, God's people—His Church—will be victorious in the end (section spanning Chapter 6:1—8:1).

CHAPTER 6

4.1 The first seal: Believers can expect to suffer in this world because of military conflict (6:1-2).

[1]As we continued to worship the One who holds all existence securely in His hands, I saw the Lamb holding the scroll containing God's plan for history. There were seven seals on the scroll, and the Lamb was about to break open the first. As each seal was broken, it unraveled a layer of God's plan. With each layer's unveiling, we are able to know God's judgments that will precede the coming of His full kingdom. Then I saw the Lamb grasp the scroll and open the first seal.

When He opened it, one of the four living creatures said to me in a thunderous voice, "Come out and hear creation's cries of longing and the global suffering that is unfolding."

[2]I looked, and there before me was a white horse. Like a victorious, military force, the symbolic white horse represented how God's judgment on the world occurs through military powers. The rider of the white horse had a bow in his hand and a crown of victory on his head. He rode out conquering everything in his path.

4.2 The second seal: Believers can expect to suffer in this world because of human conflict and confusion (6:3-4).

[3]When the Lamb opened the second seal, I heard the second living creature say, "Come out and hear creation's cries of longing and the global suffering that is unfolding."

[4]Then I saw a flaming red horse. The symbolism of the flaming red horse represented how God's judgments on the world occur through ongoing strife and confusion. The rider of the red horse had been empowered to take peace from the earth; he enticed people to kill one another. He was given a large sword, which indicated to me that he had the power to cause large amounts of strife and conflict.

4.3 The third seal: Believers can expect to suffer in this world due to a lack of resources and unmet needs (6:5-6).

[5]When the Lamb opened the third seal, I heard the third living creature say, "Come out and hear creation's cries of longing and the global suffering that is unfolding."

[6]Then I saw a black horse, which implied a scarcity of resources and death. The symbolism of the black horse represented how God's judgment on the world occurs through economic difficulties. The rider of the black horse held a pair of ancient weight scales—the kind used in commerce—in his hand.

Then I heard a voice echo throughout God's creation (symbolized by the four living creatures), saying, "Things are so bad economically that it will take you an entire day's wages to buy the bread for just one average meal—either one loaf of wheat bread or three loaves of barley. But even those who can afford to buy the bread for one meal will not have enough left to buy the oil or wine to go with it. Economic conditions will be so tough that you will not be able to buy all the food you genuinely need. Many will suffer due to the lack of resources.

4.4 The fourth seal: Believers can expect to suffer in this world because of death (6:7-8).

[7]When the Lamb opened the fourth seal, I heard the fourth living creature say, "Come out and hear creation's cries of longing and the global suffering that is unfolding."

[8]Then I saw a beaten, bruised, ashen, pale horse. The symbolism of the pale horse represented how God's judgment on the world occurs through death. The rider of the pale horse was named Death, and Hades—the realm of the dead—followed with him. They were given the power to kill one-fourth of the earth by the sword, famine, deadly diseases, and vicious wildlife.

4.5 The fifth seal: Believers can expect to suffer in this world for being faithful witnesses (6:9-11).

⁹When the Lamb opened the fifth seal, I saw underneath the altar all the martyrs—those who had been killed for living according to God's Word and for the witness their lives produced.

¹⁰These martyrs called out in a loud, unified voice, "How long, O Sovereign-Ruling Lord, do we have to wait? To the One who is whole, complete, and true, how long will it be until You decisively judge those who only live for themselves in the present world with no mindfulness toward You? When will Your eternal justice for us, Your martyrs, be completed?"

¹¹Then each of them was given a long, flowing, and pure white robe. The robe symbolized how they—even though they faced death and condemnation from the world—were justified in Christ. Their robes of Christ's righteousness (signifying a right standing before God and a right relationship with Him) were both a sign and pledge they could hold on to, for they were told they would only have to wait a little while longer. They were asked to wait until the full number of the martyred Christian men and women had reached its limit.

4.6 The sixth seal: Believers can expect to suffer in this world on the day when history ends (6:12-17).

¹²When the Lamb opened the sixth seal, I looked and saw a series of cataclysmic events that signified the end of human history. During this time, there was a great earthquake. The sun turned darker than black cloth. The entire moon turned blood red. ¹³Stars and celestial objects fell from the sky. They fell to earth as easily as a fig tree sheds its leaves when shaken by a strong wind. ¹⁴During this time, the sky vanished like a scroll that was being rolled up. Every mountain and island were uprooted from their original places.

¹⁵Then epic pandemonium set in; it struck everyone. It did not matter who you were or what your societal status was. Everyone was terrified

and tried to escape. Whether kings, princes, political leaders, army generals, the wealthy, those physically strong, or just common people—whether enslaved, in debt, or financially independent and free—everyone tried to hide in the caves and in the mountains. [16]They were all desperate to escape what was coming. They pleaded with the rocks and mountains, "Please fall all around us, trapping us, in the hopes that you may hide us from the face of the One who sits on the throne and the wrath of the Lamb! [17]For the great day of God's wrath against human sinfulness has come, and who can possibly survive it?"

CHAPTER 7

4.7 The interlude between the sixth and seventh seals: Even though suffering exists, God's people, His Church, are secure and eternally indestructible (7:1-17).

4.7.1 All of God's people are eternally secure (7:1-3).

[1]Up until now, I had seen six seals opened. But before the opening of the seventh, I saw two new visions. These new visions caused a jump in the chronology—the first vision taking place before any of the seals were ever broken and the second vision happening after all the seals had been opened and history was no more. Also, these two visions gave me a view from a different, higher level that was above human history. These visions provided with a view from God's perspective and showed me how His people are eternally sealed and secure from suffering in the world. The point of both of these visions is that God's people may go through suffering, but we do so with God's eternal signature and seal upon us, knowing that He is ultimately in control.

So, what did I actually see in this first vision from a higher level? I saw four angels standing at the four corners of the earth. They were firmly holding back the earth's four destructive winds. These four winds—like the four horsemen mentioned earlier—are powerful, destructive forces working in the world to inflict pain and suffering on many. The four angels, which represent God's spiritual power at work in the world, firmly hold these destructive spiritual winds in their place.

They ensure the destructive spiritual winds only work within allowed parameters. These angels prevent any destructive spiritual wind from affecting the earth beyond what is allowed, whether on land, in the sea, or in the air.

²As part of this first vision from a higher level, I also saw another angel. This angel was approaching from the east horizon like the rising sun. The angel was carrying the seal of the living God—the one used to mark those who belong to God and which gives them assurance of their eternal security. The angel carrying the seal called out to the other four angels, the ones monitoring the earth and with the power and authority to hold back the destructive spiritual winds at work in the world.

³The angel with the seal said to the other four, "Do not let the earth be destroyed—neither the land, sea, or sky above—until we have placed God's seal (represented by a mark on one's forehead) on all of God's people."

4.7.2 All of God's people have an equal share in His kingdom (7.4-12).

⁴As I wondered how people would be sealed with God's mark, I heard a number mentioned: 144,000. It was clear that the 144,000 was not a literal number but a symbolic representation of all who would be sealed by God, those who would be eternally secure with Him. The symbolic 144,000 conveyed to me that all of God's people would be eternally secure regardless of what tribe or people group they came from.

> ⁵It did not matter if they were from the tribe of Judah.
> A symbolic 12,000 of them were sealed to communicate that every tribe of God's people has an equal share in His kingdom.
>
> It did not matter if they were from the tribe of Reuben.
> A symbolic 12,000 of them were sealed to communicate that every tribe of God's people has an equal share in His kingdom.

It did not matter if they were from the tribe of Gad. A symbolic 12,000 of them were sealed to communicate that every tribe of God's people has an equal share in His kingdom.

6It did not matter if they were from the tribe of Asher.
A symbolic 12,000 of them were sealed to communicate that every tribe of God's people has an equal share in His kingdom.

It did not matter if they were from the tribe of Naphtali.
A symbolic 12,000 of them were sealed to communicate that every tribe of God's people has an equal share in His kingdom.

It did not matter if they were from the tribe of Manasseh.
A symbolic 12,000 of them were sealed to communicate that every tribe of God's people has an equal share in His kingdom.

7It did not matter if they were from the tribe of Simeon.
A symbolic 12,000 of them were sealed to communicate that every tribe of God's people has an equal share in His kingdom.

It did not matter if they were from the tribe of Levi. A symbolic 12,000 of them were sealed to communicate that every tribe of God's people has an equal share in His kingdom.

It did not matter if they were from the tribe of Issachar.
A symbolic 12,000 of them were sealed to communicate that every tribe of God's people has an equal share in His kingdom.

8It did not matter if they were from the tribe of Zebulun.
A symbolic 12,000 of them were sealed to communicate that every tribe of God's people has an equal share in His kingdom.

It did not matter if they were from the tribe of Joseph.
A symbolic 12,000 of them were sealed to communicate that every tribe of God's people has an equal share in His kingdom.

It did not matter if they were from the tribe of Benjamin.
A symbolic 12,000 of them were sealed to communicate that
every tribe of God's people has an equal share in His kingdom.

[9]After seeing this first vision of how God seals and secures all of His people, I saw a second vision from a higher level. Chronologically, there was another shift in time. The first vision happened before the seals were broken; this second one revealed what will happen after all the seals of the scroll have been opened, after human history is no more. It is a vision of eternity, of God's people in their full future glory eternally secure and in the presence of their Lord.

In this second vision, a great multitude of people appeared before God's throne and before the Lamb. The number was so vast and so large that it was beyond counting. This immeasurable multitude was standing before God's throne and the Lamb; it consisted of people from every nation, tribe, people group, and language.

[10]In a powerful, unified voice, they cried out:

> "Our salvation comes from our God.
> To the One who sits on the throne, and
> To the Lamb, we owe everything."

[11]All the angels were standing around the throne, along with the twenty-four leaders (symbolizing God's Church) and the four living creatures (symbolizing God's creation). In symphonic harmony, they all bowed down with their faces to the ground and worshiped God. Together, they and the chorus of immeasurable number said in a unified voice:

> [12]"Indeed, this is true!
> Let us give all our praise and glory
> And wisdom and thanks and honor
> And Power and strength to our God,
> Forever and ever.
> Truly, He is worthy of it all, and always will be!"

4.7.3 All of God's people are clothed in Christ's moral
perfection and completeness of character and will never
lack anything throughout eternity (7:13-17).

¹³Then one of the twenty-four leaders, anticipating the question on my mind, asked me, "Who are all these people clothed in white robes? Where did they all come from?"

¹⁴I responded, "I would like to know, and I am confident you know the answer."

And he said to me, "All the people in white robes are those who have faithfully endured until the end, even through great affliction and suffering. Through their faith in Christ's sacrifice, their filthy, sin-stained garments have been replaced with Christ's pure, white robe of righteousness (signifying His moral completeness and right standing with God).

¹⁵"As a result of being clothed in Christ's righteousness:

"They are able to stand in God's presence before His throne.
They serve Him day and night in the place where He dwells.
And the presence of the One who sits on the throne
Shelters all those robed in righteousness and moral purity
    with eternal peace.

¹⁶"Never again will they endure hunger;
Never again will they suffer in thirst.
Never again will they burn from the sun's rays;
Never again will they suffer from the scorching heat.

¹⁷"For the Lamb on the center of the throne will be their shepherd.
He will protect them and provide for all their needs;
He will lead them to springs of living water that fulfills their
    longing for spiritual wholeness.
Like children delivered from crying sorrow to joyful delight,
God will wipe away every tear from their eyes and replace those
    tears with everlasting sights of joy."

CHAPTER 8

4.8 The seventh seal: Believers can expect some things about God's full kingdom to remain a marvelous mystery until Christ comes again (8:1).

[1]After seeing these two visions, I understood their point—that God's people may experience suffering in the world, but we can have absolute assurance that God is in control and provides us with eternal security. Having understood and seen these visions from a higher spiritual view, I was brought back down to the vision of the seven seals. The first five seals made me aware of how suffering will exist throughout human history. The sixth seal gave me a glimpse of the great, cataclysmic events that will end human history. I had seen the Lamb open the first six seals, but one remained.

When He opened the seventh seal, I did not see anything. There were no details about what life with God will be like when time and history has ended. Instead, when the seventh seal was opened, there was only silence in heaven for half an hour. The silence spoke powerfully to me. It signified the future mystery of realities that, for now, remain unknown and unseen.

We all sat in silence for about half an hour as we honored the marvelous mystery of God's full kingdom and its future arrival. After the period of humble silence, the vision of the seven seals concluded.

5. The seven trumpets: Even though suffering will exist in this world throughout history, it serves a divine purpose (section spanning Chapter 8:2—11:19).

5.1 Introduction to the seven trumpets: Everyone can expect suffering in this world (8:2-5).

5.1.1 God allows suffering in the world, and it serves a larger, divine purpose (8:2).

²Though the vision of the seven seals had concluded, there were more visions God wanted me to see. He wanted to show me another perspective, another facet, of the same reality they had just shown me. The vision of the seven seals had focused on the security of God's people as they experience suffering in the world. But now He wanted me to see: 1) how suffering will come to the entire world in general and 2) the special, divine purpose it serves.

In this new vision, I saw seven angels who were standing before the altar that stands in God's presence ready to do His work. They were given seven trumpets. These were the seven trumpets of God's judgment that will precede the coming of His kingdom. They describe the same judgment as the seven seals—just from another angle.

5.1.2 God allows suffering in the world, but He hears His people's prayers for justice and reveals His active judgment against evil (8:3-5).

³As I watched, I saw another angel come to the altar that stands in God's presence. This incense altar before the great throne is where people's prayers come before God. As this angel stood over the altar, he had a golden censer in his hand. In Old Covenant religious practices, a censer was a tool used to grab a burning hot coal and place it on an altar. When incense was poured on the burning coal, it would create a pleasing smoke-filled aroma that symbolically ascended to God.

This angel in front of the altar had a golden censer in his hand. He was given an abundance of fragrant incense to pour over the burning coals, which were the prayers of God's people. Pouring the incense over the burning coals composed of people's prayers would create a pleasing aroma that would rise from the golden altar in front of God's throne.

⁴As the angel used the golden censer and mixed these elements on the golden altar, the prayers of God's people produced a pleasing, smoke-filled aroma that rose before God.

⁵After creating the pleasing aroma from people's prayers, the angel then took the censer and performed another action. He filled the censer with the fire that was burning on the altar and threw it upon the earth. Accompanying this fire of judgment came rolling thunder, rumbling skies, flashes of lightning, and an earthquake. This action demonstrated that the prayers of God's people for justice and judgment had been heard and were fulfilled.

5.2 The first trumpet: Everyone can expect to suffer in this world because God's active judgment against evil allows powerful forces to destroy part of humanity's environment (8:6-7).

⁶Then I saw the seven angels holding the seven trumpets, prepared to release their mighty sound.

⁷The first angel blew his trumpet. Upon its sound, a hailstorm and a great fire were thrown upon the earth. Their destructive power shed much blood. A third of the earth was completely burned; a third of the trees were burned down; and all the green grass was scorched. Hearing this first trumpet revealed that God's judgment is active in the world by allowing powerful forces to destroy part of humanity's environment.

5.3 The second trumpet: Everyone can expect to suffer in this world because of God's active judgment against evil affects and destroys part of humanity's commerce (8:8-9).

⁸The second angel blew his trumpet. Upon its sound, something like a huge volcano was thrown into the sea. It turned one-third of the sea into a pool of blood, and this pool of blood reminded me of the first plague during the exodus from Egypt. ⁹This judgment killed one-third

of all marine life and wiped out one-third of all ships. Hearing the second trumpet revealed that God's judgment is active in the world by affecting and destroying part of humanity's commerce.

5.4 The third trumpet: Everyone can expect to suffer in this world because God's active judgment against evil allows part of humanity's resources for living to be destroyed (8:10-11).

[10]The third angel blew his trumpet. Upon its sound, a huge star, blazing like a torch, fell from the sky. Its impact wiped out one-third of the rivers and one-third of the springs. The result of its impact caused one-third of the earth's waters to have a bitter taste—[11]hence they called this star Wormwood because of the bitterness it produced. A third of the world's water was undrinkable. It was bitter, diseased, and caused many who drank it to die. Hearing the third trumpet revealed that God's judgment is active in the world by destroying part of humanity's resources for living.

5.5 The fourth trumpet: Everyone can expect to suffer in this world because God's active judgment against evil allows part of humanity's ability to see to be destroyed (8:12-13).

[12]The fourth angel blew his trumpet. Upon its sound, something happened that I could not explain. I do not know how it happened; I only know who did it and what it meant. This trumpet's sounding caused one-third of the universe's light to be lost as one-third of the sun, one-third of the moon, and one-third of the stars were blacked out. The result: one-third of the world was covered in darkness. One-third of the earth experienced a daytime and nighttime without any light. Hearing this fourth trumpet revealed that God's judgment is active in the world by destroying part of humanity's ability to see.

[13]As I watched the events of this trumpet vision unfold, I saw an eagle flying in the space between the heavenly realm and the earth. The eagle called out in a loud voice, "Be tragically sad! Be traumatically heartbroken! Be tremendously disturbed you inhabitants of the earth!

Why? Because these were just the first four trumpets of God's judgment! These first four were directed at the world in general. Three more trumpets are yet to come! These last three trumpets will be directly focused on those who do not believe, and they will be much worse than the others. These last three trumpets will cause three devastating woes on unbelievers."

CHAPTER 9

5.6 The fifth trumpet reveals the first great terror: Everyone can expect to suffer in this world because, as history approaches its end, God will allow agents of destruction to be released upon the earth (9:1-12).

¹The fifth angel blew his trumpet. Upon its sound, I saw a fallen angel (represented by a star) that had been thrown from the heavenly realms down to the earth. God gave the fallen angel a key that would open the Abyss. This Abyss—and its chaotic waters—symbolically represented the source of evil powers in the world that were in opposition to the powers of the heavens. ²The fallen angel used the key and opened the Abyss. When he did, a great cloud of smoke poured out from the opening. It looked as though a gigantic furnace in the Abyss had produced it. As the smoke cloud continued to pour out of the Abyss, it darkened the sun and the sky. It also generated an ominous feeling, as though it were masking the arrival of an evil force.

³And that is exactly what happened next—the first devastating woe on unbelievers was released. Out of the great cloud of smoke came an army of evil locusts. But these were not just normal locusts that eat plant life. They were demonic locusts with scorpion-like stinging abilities that could venomously affect human beings. ⁴They were told not to harm any of the earth's plant life such as grass, plants, or trees. Instead, they were directed to harm only those who do not have God's seal on their foreheads. The entire scene reminded me of the plague of locust that preceded the exodus from Egypt. Much like that event, these demonic locusts were only allowed to inflict punishment on those who did not belong to God.

⁵These demonic locusts were not allowed to kill people. They were permitted to torture people for five months. The five months mentioned was not intended to be an exact amount of time. Instead, it symbolically meant the demonic locusts could torture unbelieving people for a long, set period of time. Unfortunately, their torture was not limited to just five months. And when these demonic, scorpion-like locusts stung people, they suffered severe agony—deep pain throughout their bodies, restricted and difficult breathing, tingling sensations across their skin, and swelling.

⁶During this long period of time when the demonic locusts are given freedom to torture and inflict suffering, people will seek out death to relieve their misery but will not find it. The pain and agony will be so great that people will prefer to die rather than endure it, but they will not die. Many people will live in this horrible suffering.

⁷The demonic locusts were clearly ready to fulfill their terrible and agonizing mission, and their appearance was terrifying. They looked like gigantic, powerful, and demonic warhorses ready for battle. On their heads were crowns of gold, which symbolized how they would successfully complete their mission. Their faces resembled some kind of twisted distortion between a human face and the face of a demonic beast.

⁸These demonic locusts had hair as long as a woman's (and, at the time of my writing, the length of one's hair often signals strength). Their teeth appeared as ferocious as a lion's. ⁹These demonic locusts had breastplates that seemed to be made of iron, implying that nothing could hurt them. When they moved their wings, it sounded like a thunderous herd of horses and chariots rushing into battle. ¹⁰These demonic locusts had long tails with stingers just like a scorpion. They were able to inflict agony and suffering on people for a long period of time.

¹¹These demonic and terrifying locusts were led out of the Abyss by a demonic political and military general. In Hebrew, his name is Abaddon, which means destruction. In Greek, his name is Apollyon, which means destroyer. The Apollyon name is an ironic reference

symbolizing another political and military power. The emperors of Rome like to think they were empowered by the Greek god Apollo and liked to use the symbol of locusts to indicate how they could destroy opposing forces.

The combined symbolism of what I saw from the fifth trumpet was astonishing. Overall, the point was clear: God will allow agents of destruction to be turned loose on people to inflict agony, torment, and suffering, and these destructive agents will be led by the ultimate destroyer. The political leaders of this world wielding military power and might—like the Roman emperors—could be one of these destructive agents or could not be. We rarely know for sure. Regardless, the point is the same: a demonic leader, an ultimate destroyer, will lead a destructive army to torment those who do not believe.

¹²The fifth trumpet, and the first devastating woe it released, is now past. Unfortunately, two others are approaching.

5.7 The sixth trumpet reveals the second great terror: Everyone can expect to suffer in this world when, at a given time, God will no longer hold back destructive forces that cause death (9:13-21).

¹³The sixth angel blew his trumpet. Upon its sound, I heard a voice speaking to the angel from the four horns of the golden altar that stands before God. It was the same golden altar mentioned earlier where the prayers of God's people are offered are offered to Him.

¹⁴I heard a solitary voice saying to the sixth angel, "Release the four angels of destruction we have been holding in captivity just outside our Eastern boundary." And with these words, the second devastating woe on unbelievers was put into motion.

¹⁵Like prisoners eager to be released, these four angels of destruction were ready to run free and wreak havoc. These four angels of destruction had been held back until now. Their destructive powers had been prepared for the exact hour, day, month, and year of God's

choosing—a time when He would release them to kill one-third of humankind. [16]These four angels of destruction led a massive demonic cavalry. The number of troops in this demonic army was too big to count. I will just throw out a huge number to paint a picture for you and say there was around two-hundred million cavalry in this demonic army. Regardless of the exact number, I got the point of what I saw—it was an overpowering demonic army that would outnumber any human army by at least twenty times over. It was a destructive military force that could not be stopped.

[17]The demonic cavalry riders and their horses looked terrifying, inconceivable, and revolting. Seeing them was one of the worst things you could ever imagine or see. I am not sure my words can describe how terrifying they looked, but I will try to paint a verbal picture of their horrible appearance for you.

These demonic riders had breastplates bearing the most unimaginable, intimidating colors possible in hues that do not even exist on earth. Yet, I was able to discern the meaning of this impossible color combination. It communicated that these riders will consume and destroy with passion. Like a raging and an uncontrollable fire, they will destroy everything in their path.

The heads on these demonic horses were also unnatural. Their heads looked like some ungodly hybrid beast that loosely resembled a lion's head. Worse, out of these demonic beasts' mouths came immense destructive power such as fire, smoke, and burning sulfur. [18]With these destructive powers that came out of their mouth, they killed one-third of the human race. The first woe of locusts brought torment and suffering, but this second woe brought death.

[19]These descriptions are not exact by any means. The terror of that army was beyond words. But it seemed like these demonic beasts had not only the power to kill from their mouth but also the power to wreak havoc and inflict injury with their tails, which also had heads! Again, words fail me, but you get the point—these fire-breathing monsters from the underworld had immense power to cause suffering and to kill.

[20]Their destructive powers killed one-third of the human race. But even after all these deaths, unfortunately, all the remaining men and women did not turn to and genuinely trust in God. Instead, they centered their lives on anything they could conjure up other than God:

- the works of their hands [new advances in science, medicine, technology, mathematics, engineering, etc.],
- their ideologies [philosophies, psychological and sociological theories, false religious beliefs, self-reliance, political beliefs, etc.], and
- their human cultural achievements [improving communication, the economy, education, business, military strategies, etc.].

They paraded these achievements as though they could solve all their problems and were of greater worth than gold, silver, and bronze. They thought their advances were indestructible, stronger than stone and more permanent than petrified wood. However, none of these false centers for living could give one true spiritual and eternal life. These false gods and idols cannot see, hear, or walk like our one, true living God. Yet the remaining human race oriented their lives and their hopes on these false gods and idols.

[21]Worse, even though they saw the terrible and tragic deaths from the previous trumpets, they did not permanently change their behaviors at all. They continued to murder, trust in magical arts, trust in powers of human achievement, participate in sexually immoral acts, and steal from others. They continued to build their lives on false religious centers. Even though these people had seen God's judgment revealed against the world in general through the first four trumpets—seeing the environment experience destruction, economic turmoil, scarcity of human resources for living, and knowing the limited vision of human beings—they still did not turn to God! Even though the remaining people still alive had seen immense suffering, torment, and agony all around them, they did not change. Even though they saw the sad and tragic deaths of others, they still did not center their lives on the One who gives true and everlasting life.

CHAPTER 10

5.8 The interlude between the sixth and seventh trumpets: Unbelievers are warned (10:1-11:14).

5.8.1 There will come a time when human history will end (10:1-4).

¹Up until now, I had seen six angels sound six trumpets. But before the seventh angel came and sounded the seventh trumpet, a mighty angel appeared and interrupted the sequence. Much like the previous jump in chronology that happened between the sixth and seventh seals, this interruption set the tone before the final climactic sound of the seventh trumpet that was to come.

This mighty angel that was setting the tone before the seventh trumpet came down to earth from the heavenly realms. As this mighty angel appeared, he was surrounded by a cloud; it looked like he was wearing it. He had a rainbow above his head that looked like a halo. His face resonated light as bright as the sun, and his legs were like pillars of fire. The entire scene of the mighty angel's arrival reminded me of the exodus event where God led His people by pillars of clouds by day and fire by night.

²The mighty angel held a small scroll-like book open in his hand. Seeing the little book open in his hand made me think of Ezekiel 2:8–3:3, a passage in which an angel showed the prophet a list of bad things that were about to happen to the unbelieving people. Then, the mighty angel planted his right foot on the sea and his left foot on the land, demonstrating his authoritative presence over both. ³As the mighty angel stood there, he called out in a thunderous roar. When his voice roared, the seven thunders (which are a figurative representation of God or Christ) responded and spoke with distinct words.

⁴As I listened to what the seven thunders had to say, I was amazed. I was about to write down what they had said, but then I heard a voice from heaven say, "Do not do that. Do not write down what we

just told you. Seal up what God (the seven thunders) has said. Those words are not supposed to be shared."

> *5.8.2 There will come a time when God's full kingdom will come (10:5-7).*

⁵Then the mighty angel whom I had seen standing with one foot on the sea and the other on the land raised his right hand to the heavens. This dramatic gesture let us know he had a message with immediate worldwide implications. ⁶He spoke as though giving an oath as a sworn witness sharing the decisive truth from the One who lives forever and ever—the One who created the heavens, the earth, the sea, and all that is in them. The mighty angel declared: "The waiting is over! There shall be no more delay! God's full kingdom is coming now! ⁷And in these last moments, right before the seventh angel blows the seventh trumpet and ushers in the full coming of God's kingdom, the sharing of God's good news in Jesus Christ—the mystery of God—will have accomplished everything it was supposed to. Just as He has announced and promised to his servants throughout the ages, God's plan will have been fulfilled."

> *5.8.3 Unbelievers must be warned of their coming doom at the ultimate end (10:8-11).*

⁸Then the voice that had spoken to me from heaven called to me once more: "Go up to the mighty angel who is standing authoritatively on the sea and the land. Do not be afraid to approach him. Take the little scroll-like book out of his hand."

⁹I did as I had been directed. I went up to the mighty angel and asked him to give me the little scroll-like book. He said to me, "Take it and eat it. It will make you sick to your stomach, but in your mouth, it will be as sweet as honey."

¹⁰I took the little scroll-like book was a record God's lamentations and judgments. I took it from the angel's hand and ate it. The little scroll-like book was exactly as he said. It tasted as sweet as honey in my mouth, but after I had eaten it, it made me sick to my stomach.

¹¹Then I realized why the little scroll-like book had such a bittersweet effect and what they wanted me to learn. I would have to experience both the joy and pain of 1) knowing God's grace and His judgment and 2) making it known to others. For after I had eaten it, I was told, "You have seen great things. Now, you must go to as many people groups, nations, languages, and leaders as you can. You must tell them what you know as though you are divinely inspired. It is vital that they all hear about the final act in God's great drama of creative and redemptive history."

CHAPTER 11

5.8.4 God's people will live with Him; unbelievers will not dwell in His presence (11:1-2).

¹After I had eaten the little scroll-like book, I was commissioned to move from a passive spectator to an active participant in this particular vision taking place between the sixth and seventh trumpets. I was given a bamboo-like measuring rod used to measure things. I was told, "Rise up and go take the measure of the figurative temple of God, the altar, and all the people who love Me in it." I understood I was being asked to take account of all the people who had faith in Christ and were a part of God's universal Church. A time of spiritual danger was approaching, and God was taking account of His people, the ones He would protect and preserve through the approaching danger.

²However, I was specifically told to exclude the temple's outer court from the measurements. The voice said, "Do not measure it because the realm outside of the universal Church has been given over to unbelieving peoples. They will dwell outside the temple's outer courts, and I will trample the holy city for 42 months." Even though the voice was talking about the symbolic meaning of the temple and Jerusalem in the Old Covenant Scriptures, I understood the broader implication—that unbelieving people will dwell outside God's Church and the earth will be trampled upon for a period of time.

5.8.5 God's people will be protected by God's power; unbelievers will be doomed (11:3-6).

³The voice continued, "I will appoint My two witnesses," which was a prophetic reference to Elijah and Moses—who, in the Old Covenant [Old Testament] Scriptures, symbolically represented all of God's witnessing people. "The truth from My two witnesses will speak to the people, urging them to turn to Me during this period of trampling. They will dress in sackcloth as they mourn the coming judgment on unbelievers.

⁴"These two witnesses—symbolically representing all people who witness to Me—are like two strong olive trees and two lampstands that stand before the Lord of the earth. Just as these olive trees and lampstands are in a prime location near Me and can convey My presence, My witnesses will speak with spiritual power and authority everywhere they go throughout the earth.

⁵"If anyone wants to harm My witnesses, they should beware. My witnesses are no less protected now by My power than those who spoke for Me in the past. Remember how Elijah was protected from his enemies by the fire that fell from heaven in 2 Kings 1? Just like My former prophets, My witnesses can protect themselves by the fire they speak, the powerful words that come from their mouths, trusting that their message of God's judgment will eventually be fulfilled through God's power.

⁶"Remember how Elijah was able to cause a drought in 1 Kings 17? My witnesses are no less powerful now. Figuratively speaking, My witnesses have the power to stop the clouds from collecting evaporated water and can effectively turn off the sky's faucet so that no rain falls. And do you remember how Moses turned the river's waters into blood in Exodus 7? My witnesses are no less powerful now. Figuratively speaking, My witnesses have the power to stop the rain, turn the waters into blood, and send any type of plague on anyone opposing them anytime they want."

5.8.6 Before the ultimate end, the Devil's workings will blind many and turn them against God and His people (11:7-10).

⁷"When My witnesses have completed their task, and human history's curtain has drawn to a close, the well-known beast will come up from the Abyss and attack God's people. The well-known beast will overpower them and kill them. ⁸Believing the beast has won a decisive victory, and in contempt for the witnesses' faith, people will allow the witnesses' dead bodies to lie exposed in the public squares of the great, leading, and culturally-important cities of our day, cities like Rome. In a spiritual sense, these great, leading, and culturally important cities will be as immoral as Sodom was in Genesis and as oppressive and abusive as Egypt was in Exodus. These great, leading, and so-called important cities will be just as spiritually dead as the city where they rejected and crucified the Lord.

⁹"For a short period of time, people from every race, people group, language, and nation will gaze at My witnesses' dead bodies. They will not even allow them to be buried in order to continue their disgrace. ¹⁰And those still living on the earth will gloat over the deaths of My witnesses. They will celebrate their deaths by giving congratulatory gifts to one another. The people of the earth will see the death of God's witnesses as a great relief. Why? Because they will no longer have to hear them—for the people of the world had come to perceive their message as intolerant, tormenting, and judgmental."

5.8.7 Unbelievers will realize they made a mistake and be filled with fear as they watch God's people be resurrected and go to dwell with God (11:11-12).

¹¹But after this short period of demonic gloating and celebration, God breathed life once again into His witnesses' dead bodies. Life—fresh, new, indestructible, and resurrected—entered them. Physically alive once more, they stood on their feet again. Terror and fearful dread spread across all who saw God's resurrected people.

¹²Then a loud voice from the heavenly realms echoed out for all to hear. The loud voice spoke to God's resurrected people, saying,

"Come up here and be with Me." And they did just that. They rose up and entered the heavenly realms in a cloud just as Moses and Elijah had done. The whole unbelieving world set against God watched it happen.

5.8.8 Unbelievers will be filled with fear of the ultimate end and experience the ultimate catastrophe (11:13-14).

[13]Then, in the very next moment, there was a catastrophic earthquake. One-tenth of the great, leading, culturally important cities of the age collapsed. A large portion—about one-tenth of the cities' populations—was killed in the earthquake. After seeing God's people resurrected and these cataclysmic events, the remaining people were filled with fear and terror. The events compelled them to give glory and honor to the God of the heavenly realms.

[14]As this unique vision that occurred between the sixth and seventh trumpets concluded, an ominous feeling set in. For the sixth trumpet, and the second devastating woe it released, was now past. But the third and last woe was quickly approaching.

5.9 The seventh trumpet reveals the third great terror: Everyone can expect an ultimate end to come, and when it does, there will be a final reward for some and a final judgment for others (11:15-19).

[15]The seventh angel blew his trumpet. Upon its sound, many mighty voices in the heavenly realms spoke in unison:

"The present experience of the sin, death, and the devil ruling
over the world is over.
The world has been transformed.
Now the total and complete kingdom of our God and his
Anointed Deliver—Jesus Christ—has come.
He shall reign forever and ever!"

[16]Then the twenty-four religious leaders (symbolizing all of God's people), who sit on their thrones before God, fell face down and worshiped him. [17]They were joyfully exclaiming:

> "We give thanks to the God who has all power, to the One who
> Rules over all things, and to the Almighty God who always was
>   and who will always be.
> You have always been sovereign and in control. But now You
>   have brought Your full kingdom to the earth. Your total and
>   complete reign is now fully known, and we all experience it.
>
> [18]"The nations—and all the people of the world in them—
>   conspired, plotted, and raged against Your rule over and in
>   their lives.
> But your wrath has come.
> The point of no return has passed. It is too late now.
> The time has come for three decisive actions.
> First, the time has come for judging those who did not place
>   their faith in Christ.
> Second, the time has come for rewarding both 1) those who
>   were specifically called to be a prophetic voice to their
>   culture and 2) all the faithful believers who lived to honor
>   the Lord—no matter how well-known they were.
> Third, the time has come for destroying those who had a sinful,
>   destructive presence during their time on earth."

[19]With the seventh trumpet sounded, I was shown another aspect of God's judgment on the world. I was shown the cosmic conflict that has been happening throughout history, occurring in the spiritual realm in the air around us.

In order to see it, the doors to God's cosmic temple were opened. The temple, in the Scriptures of the Old Covenant [Old Testament], represented the place where God dwells, and, unlike the Jewish Temple from the Old Covenant, I was being brought into a place behind the spiritual veil that covers this world, gaining a glimpse into the cosmic conflict that is happening in the air around us.

And in God's cosmic temple (the spiritual realm where God dwells in perfection that is veiled in the air around us), I saw the ark of God's covenant. Its presence clearly communicated that God's real, intimate, full, and perfect presence was in this spiritual realm. This sight and its full meaning were overwhelming. Imagine the fearful awe of experiencing all of these things at the same time: flashes of lightning filling the sky, loud rumblings echoing all around, thunder rolling through the clouds, a great hailstorm, and the earth shaking below your feet.

Seeing behind the spiritual veil of our existence—being in God's cosmic temple and in the midst of His full presence—was more fearfully awe-inspiring than all of these things combined. It was beyond amazing and better than words can describe. Beyond imagination. And all of it was just a prelude to the vision I was about to see—the drama of the cosmic, spiritual conflict that has been happening throughout history.

6. The drama of history: Even though suffering will exist in this world (because of the conflict between the church and the powers of evil), God's people will be victorious through Christ (section spanning Chapter 12:1–15:4).

CHAPTER 12

6.1 Introduction to the drama: Recognize the cosmic, spiritual conflict occurring throughout history's drama (12:1-17).

6.1.1 Realize there is a spiritual conflict occurring throughout history's drama, and it revolves around three primary characters: God's people, Satan, and Christ (12:1-6).

[1]As I stood in the spiritual realm that occurs in the air around human existence, a sign foreshadowing a deeper spiritual drama appeared. This deeper spiritual drama played out among three primary characters.

The first character was a woman, clothed with sunlight, standing on the moon, and wearing a tiara with twelve stars on her head. The imagery was powerful and communicated to me that: God's Church (this woman) was clothed with an all-surpassing value, beauty, and brilliance (sunlight). It also communicated to me that God's people have a permanent stature (i.e., standing on the moon). Even the twelve-star tiara (or crown) was significant, as it was a play on words referring to testimony upon which God's people rely—both the 12 tribes of Israel in the Scriptures of the Old Covenant [Old Testament] and the 12 apostles of God's New Covenant through Christ [New Testament]. And the significance of this woman (God's Church) did not stop there.

²The woman (symbolizing God's people) was pregnant, which meant God's people were full of anticipation for God's ultimate deliverance and salvation. She (referring to God's people) cried out in pain and experienced suffering as she was waiting to give birth. All of this woman's experience was a prelude to what was about to happen—the Savior was about to be born into the world to bring salvation.

³Then, onto the heavenly stage in the air around us and into this spiritual drama, the second primary character emerged. This character's presence was also a sign foreshadowing a deeper spiritual reality. The character was a gigantic, monstrous, red dragon, which symbolized the Devil, Satan. This monstrous red dragon (the Devil) had seven heads with seven crowns, which symbolized Satan's intimidating power and authority to rule over others. He also had ten horns on his head implying the terrifying strength he possessed. And the Devil, that monstrous red dragon, was about to wield his destructive power.

⁴The monstrous red dragon's tail swept across the sky. It dragged down one-third of the stars and flung them to earth. The red dragon (symbolizing Satan) did not literally tear down the stars, but I got the point: Satan has tremendous and fearful power like one who can pull down the stars.

Even though Satan, that red dragon, had immense power, he was fearful of the third primary character, who would come from the tribe of Judah—the God-child. The dragon carefully watched the woman (symbolizing God's people), hoping he might discover when the prophesied child would come. The dragon wanted to devour this God-child the moment He took on flesh and was born into the world.

⁵But the dragon was unsuccessful. Out of the woman (symbolizing God's people) came a male child who was born to fulfill God's plans. This God-child would be a Savior who—as mentioned in Psalm 2:9— "will rule over all the people and guide them with an iron scepter." I understood that the iron scepter (or staff) symbolizes the Savior's unyielding guidance and just rule. Even though the dragon (referring to Satan) tried to thwart God's plan, the Christ-child was snatched up to be with God—which was a reference to Jesus' ascension—where He rules over all things from His heavenly throne. ⁶With the God-child (meaning Christ) now ruling from the heavenly realm where God exists in perfection, I then saw another image: the woman fleeing into the desert where she found a refuge prepared for her by God where she would be taken care of for forty-two months. This is what the image I saw meant: believers will find safety and provision among the church. Throughout history, they have.

6.1.2 Realize that the drama's deeper plot reveals victory for God's people through Christ (12:7-16).

⁷With these primary characters introduced in this heavenly drama, the deeper plot was revealed. These characters were all a part of a larger, unseen, epic battle in the spiritual realm. Also, in this battle was an archangel named Michael and his army of angels. They fought against the dragon (meaning the Devil) and his demonic forces. ⁸But the demon and his army were not strong enough to stand against the archangel and his army. They were defeated and clearly did not belong in God's heavenly realm of perfection. ⁹The great dragon was cast down and thrown out—that ancient serpent known as the Devil or Satan, the one who deceives people all over the world and leads them astray. The Devil and all his demon angels were thrown down to the earth.

[10]When this happened, and God was victorious, I heard a loud voice in the heavenly realm of God's perfection, saying:

"Now God's salvation and power have been established.
The kingdom of our God and the authority of Christ have come.
The accuser of our brothers and sisters—the one who day and
    night brings charges against them before God—has been
    cast out.

[11]"God's people triumphed over their accuser, the Devil, by the
    blood of God's sacrificial Lamb and by living a life of faith
    that was a testimony to Him.
Even when faced with death, if they lived for Christ, they did
    not value their physical life as more important than living
    by faith in Him.

[12]"Therefore, rejoice! All you who live in the heavenly realm of
    God's perfection, celebrate and be glad!
But to all who live on the earth and the sea, watch out! You will
    experience a state of intense hardship because the Devil
    dwells among you!
He knows he only has a short time to dwell on the earth.
    His anger burns because of it. So watch out for the Devil."

[13]After hearing this song, the drama resumed. When the dragon (meaning the Devil) realized that he could no longer harm the Christ-child and that he had been cast down to the earth, he went after the woman (symbolizing God's people) the Christ-child came from.

[14]Even though the dragon pursued her, the woman (meaning God's people) was given two mighty eagle's wings, which symbolized God's power to deliver and protect them from harm. With these mighty eagle's wings, the woman, referring to God's people, could fly away from the serpent to a secure desert retreat God prepared for her. She (referring to the Church) would be able to rest there safely out of harm's way until the dragon's (meaning the Devil's) allotted time to accuse, harm, and persecute others was over.

¹⁵The serpent-dragon was furious. He spewed a torrent of water toward the woman (symbolizing God's people) that flowed like a wild, raging river, intending to overpower and kill them. ¹⁶But she (meaning the Church) was protected. God used the earth to protect the woman. As the torrent waters approached, the dry desert grounds absorbed all the water the dragon had spewed from his mouth.

> 6.1.3   Realize that Satan is operating a full-scale war against God's people (12:17).

¹⁷The dragon (symbolizing Satan) was furious at the woman (meaning God's people). With his plans having failed, he went away to plan a full-scale war against all her offspring—on those who follow God's teachings and hold firm in their living witness to Jesus.

CHAPTER 13

6.2 The beast out of the sea: Recognize there are political, economic, and societal factors working against God's people in this world (13:1-10).

¹As I stood on the seashore, I saw seven visions of this great, cosmic, and spiritual battle. Standing there, I saw the first vision—the dragon conducting the next phase of his battle plan by raising a ferocious beast up out of the sea. This sea-beast symbolized the political powers that work against us in this world. He had ten horns (symbolizing his great strength) and seven heads (representing his strong authority). On his ten horns, the sea-beast had ten crowns (symbolizing his political rule). And written on each of the seven heads were titles for the common thoughts that often lead people to blasphemy—that lead people to trust in themselves instead of God.

²Do you remember the four beasts prophesied in Daniel 7? This one ferocious sea-beast is all four of those beasts fearfully combined into one. The sea-beast seemed as agile and cunning as a leopard, possessed feet as strong and mighty as a bear, and had a mouth as powerful and forceful as a lion. Even though he was ferocious, the sea-beast only

had whatever power the dragon (symbolizing Satan) gave him. The dragon gave the sea-beast the same power and authority to destroy that he possessed. [3]Even though this sea-beast (meaning the destructive political powers) appeared to die of a fatal wound, it did not die or pass away. Instead, it healed itself and resurfaced as a powerful force once again. The whole world was amazed and admired the sea-beast's political resurrection. The world marveled at the power he wielded, and many people began following the sea-beast.

[4]The sea-beast (meaning the powers that be) deceived, lied, and manipulated the people with his great power. People began to worship the dragon (meaning the Devil) because they had seen the sea-beast's political power and authority. People of the world also praised and worshiped the sea-beast because of his ability to rule. The people asked, "Is there anyone who can govern and care for the world the way the sea-beast has done? No one can do better than the sea-beast. Is there anyone who would dare to go to war against him? They would surely be defeated."

[5]The sea-beast also possessed a powerful ability to communicate. He was able to speak proud, boastful words that persuaded people of his God-like qualities, which was a direct blasphemy against God. The sea-beast was allowed by God to exercise his devilish authority throughout human history, but his reign would be a short time compared to eternity.

[6]The sea-beast (symbolizing the political powers in the world) did exactly what he was allowed to do. He communicated slanderous accusations against God. He did everything in his power to persuade people to follow anything other than God. He made God, the idea of being with God in the heavenly realm of his perfection, and anyone who lived for Christ looks like villainous forces working against the good of the world. [7]Deriving power from the dragon (symbolizing Satan), the sea-beast had the ability to wage war against the followers of Christ—God's holy people. In many cases, the sea-beast could overpower and conquer God's people. The sea-beast, with his conniving powers, was able to infiltrate, persuade, and wield authority within every tribe, people group, language, and nation of the world.

⁸People from all across the earth will worship the sea-beast in one form or another. That is every person except those whose names are written down in the Lamb's book of life (referring to where God keeps a record of those who are truly His followers). Christ's followers know that God's sacrificial Lamb was slain from the creation of the world on their behalf. They will not follow or give their allegiance to the sea-beast (referring to his societal or political power or influence). Everyone else may—in one form or another—but not Christ's followers.

⁹Whoever has ears should use them to listen. You know the sea-beast (referring to the societal and political powers that be) is operating in the midst of human history. What should you do? Here is a wise saying that we would do well to follow:

> ¹⁰"If the powers that be take you captive, then peacefully go
> into captivity.
> Even if the powers that be conspire against you to take your
> physical life, then do not be afraid to let them have it."

That is a very tough calling, I know. But as God's people, we are called to remain faithful. We are called to endure patiently no matter what the Devil and the world may throw at us.

6.3 The beast out of the earth: Recognize there are false religions that lead people astray (13:11-15).

¹¹After seeing the full intention of the sea-beast (referring to the political and societal powers that be), I then saw the second vision of the cosmic, spiritual conflict—the second beast. This second beast was coming up from the abyss and out of the earth. This land-beast had two horns (symbolizing his power, might, and character). His horned appearance made him look like a lamb (meaning God's agent), but the land-beast's deceptive, conniving, and lying communication showed him to serve the dragon's purposes, not God's.

[12]Even though he was ferocious, the land-beast—which symbolized false religion that led people astray—only had whatever power he derived from the dragon (symbolizing Satan). The dragon gave the land-beast the same power and authority to destroy that he possessed. The land-beast persuaded the people of the earth to worship the sea-beast (meaning the societal and political powers that be) because of the revived, resurfaced power he was displaying.

[13]The land-beast (symbolizing false religion) performed great signs and wonders to draw people in. He even reproduced an act of an Old Covenant [Old Testament] prophet, calling for fire to fall from the sky and land on earth in full view of everyone. [14]Since the land-beast was given the power to perform these signs and to point people toward the sea-beast (meaning the powers that be), he was able to deceive many people on earth. The land-beast led the people to worship the objects and ideologies of the sea-beast. He led them to worship anything that embodied his deceptive power, promises, and abilities.

[15]The land-beast (symbolizing false religion) had the persuasive power to invigorate and give life to the movement the sea-beast (meaning the powers that be) ignited. The land-beast managed the public relations image of the sea-beast. He used it to persuade people to kill anyone who refused to give their complete allegiance to the sea-beast.

6.4 The mark of the beast: Recognize that those who are led astray by Satan reflect him and are not safe in the cosmic, spiritual conflict (13:16-18).

[16]The land-beast (symbolizing false religion) also forced all people— both the small and the great, both the wealthy and the poor, both the free and the captive—to receive an identifying mark on their right hand and their foreheads. This identifying mark allowed them to know who followed the dragon and his beasts and who did not. [17]This identifying mark was the name of the beast, or more acutely, his name represented by numbers. In the time that I am writing this, names are sometimes represented by a number obtained by adding together the numerical value of the letters in their name. This numerical value is

often used as a symbol or mark to represent the person's name. The
land-beast forced all people to take this identifying mark. Anyone
who did not have it would suffer economic hardship among other
things. They would not be able to buy and sell goods unless they had
the land-beast's mark.

¹⁸God's people should apply wisdom here and do the math. Look at
the number of the beast and see whose name, when transliterated into
numbers, totals 666. Then you will know who you need to be on the
lookout for. In the time that I am writing this, the 666 mark refers
specifically to Nero, the Roman Emperor vehemently persecuting
God's people. But throughout history, there will be rulers and leaders
symbolically bearing 666. There will always be pseudo-christ figures
who fall short of being the Savior of the world, even if they think they
do not. Use wisdom and be on the lookout for these agents of the
dragon (meaning the Devil) throughout history.

CHAPTER 14

6.5 The 144,000: Recognize that those who follow Christ reveal Him and are secure in the cosmic, spiritual conflict (14:1-5).

¹The effect of the dragon, his beasts, and those bearing his mark may
seem discouraging, but let me tell you what I saw next. It is very
encouraging for Christ's followers! I looked and saw God's sacrificial
Lamb standing on Mount Zion (a symbolic place long associated with
God's divine deliverance).

With the Lamb were a symbolic number of people (symbolized by
144,000) who had God's identifying mark on them—the name of
Christ and his Father's name written on their foreheads. Just like
before, the 144,000 was a way to represent all of God's people symbolically through a number. It did not matter what tribe or people
group they came from. Those bearing the identifying mark of Christ
were sealed by God and eternally secure with Him.

[2]I also heard a powerful voice from the heavenly realm of God's perfection. It sounded like a mighty, rushing waterfall or continually rolling thunder. Even though the sound was humbling, due to its sheer power, it also had a profound beauty to it. The sound was as eloquent and as beautiful as instruments in a well-orchestrated, grand symphony.

[3]And then the voices of God's people sang a new song. This new song had a beauty about it that transcended any earthly song ever heard. They sang this new song before God's throne, before the four living creatures (representing God's creation) and the leaders (representing all of God's people). They were celebrating God's victory. The song required such an amazing spiritual skill, character, and composition that only the 144,000 (meaning all of God's people) who had been redeemed through Christ could learn the song and carry its tune.

[4]What kind of virtue and character did these 144,000 (symbolically representing all of God's people) have that allowed them to learn this song and carry its tune? First, they faithfully followed the Lord. Figuratively, they did not defile themselves with the immoral woman that would lead them to impurity. I understood this figurative reference to the immoral woman to mean that the faithful did not pursue worldly, sinful things, because it would lead to a mixed moral character. By avoiding the immoral woman, they (meaning God's people) remained morally pure, like virgins. I understood this reference to mean they were pure in their faith, fidelity, and commitment to the Lord.

Second, they followed God's sacrificial Lamb wherever He led them. Third, they clearly had been purchased from the world's population, and they had only God and the Lamb as their owner.

[5]Lastly, no lies came out of their mouths. Unlike those who were following the dragon (the Devil), those who followed God were morally spotless before His throne.

6.6 The angels of grace, doom, and warning: Recognize that how one lives in this life will produce its proper reward after the cosmic, spiritual conflict has ended (14:6-14).

⁶With God's people clearly marked and fully belonging to Him, I then saw three angels appear. These three angels gave final warnings and final pleas for the dragon's followers to turn to the Lord. The first angel was flying, hovering between the spiritual realm in the air around us and the earth. He carried the eternal Good News that was to be proclaimed to all people—every nation, tribe, language, and people group.

⁷He pleaded with a loud voice: "Realize who God is and honor Him. Realize His all-surpassing value and worth because the impending hour of His judgment has come. Ascribe all your praise, adoration, and devotion to the One who made the earth—its skies, land, seas, and springs."

⁸Then, the second angel appeared right after the first and said, "Fallen and ruined! Utterly devastated and desolate is Babylon the Great (symbolizing how human political, religious, and societal powers can serve themselves and work against God in the world)! The perceived 'greatness' of Babylon has deceived many and seduced them into following their ways. Its intoxicating and immoral influence has lured many nations into its desolate and fallen state. But the cup of God's wrath shall come upon Babylon and upon all those following its deceptive, self-serving ways."

⁹The last of the three angels appeared after the first two. He said in a powerful voice, "If anyone devotes themselves to the sea-beast (meaning the powers that be that serve Satan), what the sea-beast represents, and lives a life consistent with the beast's identifying mark that is on them, ¹⁰then they will drink from the undiluted wine of God's fury. God has poured His full strength and wrathful power out into a cup. It is beyond pure and undiluted—700 percent proof wrath of God. Anyone devoted to the beast will drink from this fearful cup of God's wrath.

"And do you remember how Sodom and Gomorrah were destroyed with burning sulfur? People devoted to the beast will be tormented with a destruction worse than Sodom and Gomorrah. They will be tormented in the full view of God's holy angels and of the Lamb. The tormented will both glimpse God's glorious wonders that they have missed and suffer the universally public shame of their fallen choices.

[11]"And this torment will not be temporary. The smoke of their burning agony will rise forever and ever. There will be no intermission or timeout to their suffering. Day and night, they will be unrelentingly tormented. It will come upon all those who were devoted to the sea-beast and what he represented, and lived a life reflecting they had received the beast's identifying mark."

[12]The meaning of these strong warnings was clear to me. In the face of temptation, compulsion, or persuasion to follow the beast, God's people must patiently endure whatever comes their way. They must remain faithful. They must continue to follow God's teachings regardless of what may come.

[13]Then I heard an affirming voice from the heavenly realm say, "Write down this reassuring note: those who have a divine sense of fulfillment—those blessed by God—are the ones who faithfully serve Him throughout their life until their dying day."

"Yes, indeed," affirmed God's Spirit. "Those who have faithfully followed Me until their death will receive rest from their labors. The good things they did in life will not be forgotten. They will be known, remembered, and appreciated throughout eternity."

6.7 The harvesting of the earth: Recognize Christ will come again at the end of the cosmic, spiritual conflict and bring God's final judgment (14:14-2).

[14]With the 144,000 (symbolizing God's people) clearly marked and the three angels having sounded their last warnings to those following the beast, I then saw two more visions of God's judgment—one was a

vision of harvesting ripe wheat, and the other was of harvesting grapes in a winepress. Both visions were harvesting themed.

In the first one, I saw a mysterious, white, heavenly cloud approaching with a person sitting on it resembling the Son of Man. It was how the Messiah was predicted to arrive in Daniel 7:13-14. He wore a victor's crown on His head and had a harvester's sickle in His hand.

[15]Then, an angel came out of God's cosmic temple like a public address announcer. He was about to make an epic statement to the One sitting on the cloud that would be so loud the entire universe could hear. He said, "Take your harvester's sickle and reap. The time for God's great gathering of His people has come. The earth is ripe with believers and ready to be harvested." [16]The Son of Man was sitting on the cloud. He swung His harvester's sickle over the earth, and the believing people of the earth were harvested.

[17]Then I saw a second vision of God's judgment that followed the first one. In the second vision, I saw another angel come out of God's cosmic temple in the spiritual realm around us. He also had a sharp harvesting sickle in his hand.

[18]Then, I saw yet another angel emerge from the altar in front of God's throne. This angel managed and had authority over the fire that burned on God's altar (the place where people's prayers were offered up to God). The altar-managing angel spoke like a public address announcer making a loud, epic statement to the angel with the harvesting sickle. He said, "Take your sharp harvesting sickle and use it to gather all the clusters of grapes (meaning unbelieving people) from the earth's vine, for the grapes are ripe and ready for harvest."

[19]The angel with the harvesting sickle swung it on the earth. He gathered all the grapes (meaning unbelieving people) and threw them into the great winepress of God's wrath and judgment. [20]The grapes in the winepress were trampled upon in a place outside of God's city. The grapes' red juice (symbolizing the blood of unbelieving people) flowed out of the winepress of God's judgment. There was so much juice (meaning blood) that it splattered everywhere. The amount of juice

produced by the winepress of God's judgment was so deep that the tallest of horses could not walk in it. The juice, or blood, was abundant and all-pervasive; it spread out so widely that no human beings anywhere could escape God's judgment.

CHAPTER 15

6.8 The seven plagues appear: Recognize how terrible God's judgment will be for unbelievers once the cosmic, spiritual conflict ends (15:1).

[1]Then I saw something else. I saw another sign of deep, great, and ominous spiritual significance appear in the heavenly realm. I saw seven angels who held the seven last plagues of God's judgment in their hands. These seven plagues describe the same event as the seven seals and seven trumpets. The seven plagues, however, represent the last facet of God's judgment that He wants us to know about. These seven plagues reveal God's judgment on the entire world. After we see them, the picture of God's judgment will be complete, and God's warning to the world will be finished. All that will remain is the final judgment.

6.9 The victorious by the sea of glass: Recognize that God's people can celebrate victory at the end of the cosmic, spiritual conflict because of what Christ has done (15:2-4).

[2]In addition to these seven plagues of God's judgment, I saw the most amazing sea I had ever seen. Its waters were so clear and magnificent that it looked like a sea of glass. But it was more than just clear waters. It not only reflected light, but it also blended together with the amazing light around it. The effect: it looked like a sea of glass that was on fire! It was a marvelous sight.

And standing beside this magnificent sea were those who had been victorious over the sea-beast—God's followers whose lives looked like His and not like the sea-beast (referring to the Devil's agents). All

of the people victorious through Christ were there and held special
musical instruments He had given to them.

³They sang the Lamb's victory song, which was similar to Moses' victory song in Exodus 15. They sang:

> "Mighty and marvelous are the things You have done,
>   Lord God Almighty.
> Just and true are Your ways, for You are the King of the nations.
>
> ⁴"Who will not fear you, Lord? Who will not honor and value
>   living for You above all other things?
> You and Your greatness alone are set apart from the world.
>   You surpass anything else on the earth.
> All nations will come and worship before You,
> Because Your just and righteous acts have been made known.
>   They have been displayed for all to see."

7. The seven cups of God's wrath: Even though
   suffering will exist in this world, God's judgment will
   be unleashed on it and bring it to an end (section
   spanning Chapter 15:5—16:21).

   7.1 Introduction to the seven cups: The time of opportunity has
   passed; the time for God's judgment has come (15:5-8).

⁵After I had seen this amazing sea of glass and heard the song, I looked
and saw the opening of this completely new scene. This scene would
reveal to me the seven plagues that displayed the final aspect of God's
judgment.

In this new scene, I again saw God's temple in heaven, and its doors
were wide open. I did not just see the exterior of the temple. Instead,
I saw inside it. I saw something more vital and more intimate—I saw
the tent of meeting. The symbolism of seeing the tent of meeting

was not lost on me, for in the Scriptures of the Old Covenant [Old Testament], the tent of meeting was important. It was the actual place where God's presence dwelled and intersected with humanity. It was such a special place that only once a year one selected priest could enter it and be in God's presence, staying there just long enough to make an atoning sacrifice to cover the people's sins. With this Old Covenant symbolism in mind, the point was clear to me—God's righteous and just presence was there, and, because of His perfect moral standards and character, judgment was about to be executed.

⁶As I stood watching, out of the temple came seven angels. They were carrying the seven plagues of God's judgment. The seven angels wore pure white clothing that indicated they served God's noble, sacred purpose. They also wore golden sashes around their chests indicating they served a royal, priestly function.

⁷Then one of the four living creatures (representing God's creation) gave each one of the seven angels a golden cup that was full of God's indignation and wrath. There was a total of seven cups of God's wrath, and they came from the God who lives forever and ever.

⁸As the angels received these cups, the temple was filled with amazing smoke. I understood that the smoke filling the temple symbolically represented God's all-surpassing power and presence flowing over all creation. And God's presence, represented by the smoke, did not leave the temple (His creation).

His presence (symbolized by the smoke) was so overwhelming, so overpowering that no one was capable of entering the temple until the seven plagues of God's judgment had been delivered by the seven angels. The meaning was clear to me: God, in His unapproachable might and power, was making decisive actions. The time for opportunity had passed; the time for His judgment had come.

CHAPTER 16

7.2 The first cup of God's wrath: The earth experiences divine punishment (16:1-2).

¹Then I heard a mighty voice from the smoke-filled temple say to the seven angels, "Go and pour out the seven cups of God's wrath upon the earth."

²The first angel went and poured out the first cup of God's wrath on the earth. When he did, horrible, painful sores broke out on everyone who had the mark of the beast and worshipped what the beast represented.

7.3 The second cup of God's wrath: The sea experiences divine punishment (16:3).

³The second angel went and poured out the second cup of God's wrath on the sea. When he did, it turned the sea's waters into a bloody thickness. The sea looked like it was filled with the blood from dead corpses—thick, foul-smelling, and disgusting. The sea's harmful, bloody waters killed every living thing in the sea.

7.4 The third cup of God's wrath: The rivers experience divine punishment (16:4-7).

⁴The third angel went and poured out the third cup of God's wrath on the rivers and springs of water. When he did, the rivers and spring waters turned into blood.

⁵Then I heard the angel who had authority over the waters say:

"You are right and just in sending these judgments,
    O Holy One—the one who is and who has always been.
    ⁶"Since they have shed the blood of Your holy people and Your

prophets, You have given them what they deserve—blood to drink."

⁷And then I heard a voice from the altar respond:

"Yes indeed, O Lord God, the Almighty. Your judgments are true and just."

7.5 The fourth cup of God's wrath: The atmosphere experiences divine judgment (16:8-9).

⁸The fourth angel went and poured out the fourth cup of God's wrath on the sky. When he did, it melted the layers of the atmosphere. As a result, the sun's rays, in all their full force, were able to scorch everyone exposed to them.

⁹People exposed to the harsh sunlight were severely burned. They cursed the name of God because they knew He had the power to control these seven last plagues and did not stop them. But the scorched people failed to see the deeper, spiritual significance of the plagues. The seven last plagues were happening to remind people about God and to call them back to Him. Yet they did not turn from their selfish, sinful ways nor choose to live a life that ascribes all worth to God when they had the chance.

7.6 The fifth cup of God's wrath: People following Satan experience divine judgment while in this world (16:10-11).

¹⁰The fifth angel went and poured out the fifth cup of God's wrath on the sea-beast's throne (symbolizing societal and political structures of the world). When he did, it plunged the beast's evil kingdom into civil peril and darkened societal confusion. Such extreme pain, torment, and agony were experienced by the people devoted to the beast that they gnawed their own tongues. The people devoted to the beast blamed ¹¹and cursed God for their pains and sores. Yet they refused to turn to God and seek His forgiveness for the evil things they had

done. The peoples and societies following the beast's ways were in utter disarray.

7.7 The sixth cup of God's wrath: Those not living for God experience the terror of divine judgment as it nears (16:12).

¹²The sixth angel went and poured out the sixth cup of God's wrath on the mighty Euphrates river (which symbolized the region from which ultimate destruction would come). When he did, it caused the river's waters to dry up. When they dried up, it created a clear road for kings from the East to come and bring a siege of destruction upon those following the beast's ways.

7.8 The interlude between the sixth and seventh cups: Those not living for God—like the Devil and his evil forces preparing for the final battle of Armageddon—are naïve enough to think they can avoid divine judgment and stand to fight against God (16:13-16).

¹³Before the seventh angel brought the seventh cup, I saw Satan's preparations for the final cup of God's wrath. I saw three evil spirits appear, and they had a frog-like appearance. I understood the symbolism because, since the Old Covenant Scriptures, frogs were viewed as unclean and impure animals. These frog-like, impure spirits came out of the dragon's mouth (referring to the Devil), the sea-beast's mouth (referring to the society serving the Devil), and the false prophet's (or land-beast's) mouth (referring to the false religions and ideologies promoting the Devil's ways).

¹⁴These three evil spirits performed miraculous signs and wonders. These demonic, evil spirits went out to the kings, presidents, and leaders of the world and united them to make war against God, to fight in the epic battle at the end of human history—the great and terrible day when God Almighty comes.

[15]But we need to remember that we do not know when or how quickly this great day of the Lord will come. Do you remember what Jesus told us? He said, "Be on the lookout because I am going to sneak up on you like a thief. The one who stays awake and remains clothed (symbolizing being clothed in the moral purity and completeness of Christ) will experience a divine sense of fulfillment. By remaining clothed (in Christ), a person's clothes (character) will not be stolen; he or she will not be naked or shamefully exposed."

[16]Then, the dragon, his beasts, and all the leaders and people of the world gathered together to make one last, desperate effort in their war against God. They gathered for this end-game war at Armageddon—where the battle between good and evil, Christ and the Anti-Christ, and God and the Devil—would forever be decided.

7.9 The seventh cup: God's ultimate and final judgment is revealed against Satan and the world (16:17-21).

[17]The seventh angel went and poured out the seventh and last cup of God's wrath into the atmosphere. When he did, God's loud voice spoke from the throne inside the temple, saying, "It is done! All has been accomplished!"

[18]After he had declared this ultimate and final victory, bright lightning, loud rumblings, and rolling thunder filled the skies; a severe, cosmic earthquake shook the ground. This earthquake was more severe than any human had ever seen or imagined. It was so powerful that [19]it split the great city of Babylon (symbolizing the center of Satan's and the world's structure against God) into three parts. And all the cities in all the nations of the world collapsed because of this cosmic, divinely motivated earthquake. God made sure that Babylon, symbolizing the center of Satan's structure, drank the full amount from God's cup of wrath.

[20]As God's ultimate and final wrath was realized, islands were swept away; mountains disappeared and could not be found. [21]Huge hailstones weighing over 100 pounds fell from the sky and crushed

unbelieving people. These people's hearts were full of the beast's hatred of God. And the result for them: the people cursed God for the storm of His divine wrath and for the terrible experience of having to go through it.

8. An expanded vision of the seventh cup of God's wrath: Even though suffering will exist in this world, justice will be done, and evil will be destroyed (section spanning Chapter 17:1—19:10).

CHAPTER 17

8.1 The Devil's ideology will seduce many into following him (17:1-6).

¹Then, one of the seven angels who had the seven cups of God's wrath approached me. What he was about to show me was an expanded vision of the seventh cup of God's wrath and judgment—an expanded view of the seventh cup, God's judgment on Babylon. The imagery of what the angel showed me in this extended vision shifted between various symbols of evil (woman, beast, prostitute, city, king, etc.). In ancient, symbolic literature, this is normal. The point for this expanded vision of the seventh cup of God's wrath is this: all the various references are alternative ways of representing one single source and power of evil.

The angel began his expanded vision by saying, "Come with me, and I will show you the judgment of the persuasive demon prostitute (meaning the unfaithful, worldly powers that are set against God)." And I was about to see the expanded vision of their judgment during the seventh cup of God's wrath.

This demon prostitute sits beside many waters. Similar to how the Euphrates River was the source that connected ancient Babylon to the entire world and a source of its economy, this demon prostitute is wealthy because she sits at the crossroads of the world.

²She—as a source and power of evil—has influenced and persuaded many. Many rulers and leaders of the world have committed adultery with her—meaning they have been spiritually unfaithful to God because of their involvement with the evil she offers. Many people living on the earth became drunk from her wine of adultery, which means they were seduced into spiritual unfaithfulness by the allure of worldly power and influence.

³Then the angel carried me into another spiritual reality by God's Spirit. He took me to a desert-like, barren wilderness. There, I saw how evil the persuasive demon prostitute (meaning the evil, worldly powers set against God) was. I saw a woman sitting on a scarlet sea-beast, which was a reference to the ability of these evil powers against God to spread. Similar to how Roman emperors claimed to be divine, this sea-beast was covered with deceptive, blasphemous names that claimed to be gods or god-like. This sea-beast was also covered with seven heads and ten horns, which implied great authority and strength.

⁴The persuasive demon prostitute (symbolizing the source of evil) had an attractive appearance. She was dressed in purple and scarlet, glittered like gold, and wore dazzling stones and pearls. Even though she was outwardly attractive, her inward morals and character were repulsive. She held a golden cup in her hand that was full of all her evil offenses and unfaithfulness toward God. It held all the moral filth of the world, and its stench was foul and revolting.

⁵Similar to how Roman prostitutes wore headbands that had their names on them, there was a name written on the demon prostitute's forehead. It had a secret symbolic meaning that was clear to me. Her name was Babylon!

> "Babylon—the great city (which actually represented a false
>   hope and belief in a society set against God);
> Babylon—the mother of all prostitution (meaning
>   unfaithfulness toward God); and
> Babylon—the mother of all the unspeakable atrocities,
>   obscenities, and the abominable things on the earth that are
>   set against God."

⁶As I looked at the demon prostitute woman, I noticed she was drunk. She (symbolizing the worldly powers set against God) would get intoxicated by drinking the blood of God's martyred people, the blood of those who died witnessing for Christ.

When I saw the demon prostitute (representing the worldly powers set against God), her presence was so astonishingly horrible that I did not know what to think of it. I could not comprehend how horrible she is.

8.2 The Devil's ideology and the many who have been seduced into following it will be destroyed (17:7-18).

⁷But then the angel said to me, "Why are you so perplexed? I will show you the secret symbolic meaning of this astonishingly horrible woman, the seven-heads (representing worldly authority), ten horns (symbolizing worldly strength), and the beast that she rides.

⁸"The beast you saw has pseudo-Christ-like qualities and brings them to the places where we live. The beast's devilish presence has ebbed and flowed throughout human history. The beast has been present in the past. He exists in our present (even if we do not notice him "in the moment"). And you can rest assured the beast will be present in the future as well. Even though we know the beast's final, eternal fate—even though we know he is destined for eternal perdition in a lake of fire—until then, we know the beast has come up out of the Abyss and will be working in our world to destroy us.

People whose names have not been recorded in the book of life may turn to the beast and the devilish ways he inspires. The beast will captivate many people when they see him because of his pseudo-Christ-like abilities.

What are these pseudo-Christ-like abilities? There will come a time when the demonic woman's influence to turn people against God will lose its power from the world's scene. However, she will reappear once again, like a resurrection of sorts. Many people will turn away from

God and will be drawn to the beast because of his perceived pseu-
do-resurrection—his seemingly God-like ability to conquer death and
time.

[9]For those who have God's wisdom, here is a cryptic clue with meaning for our present and future. It consists of three parts. The first part
of the cryptic clue: *the seven heads are seven hills on which the woman is
sitting.* When I deciphered the cryptic clue, I quickly understood the
immediate, present reference. Rome, which is ruling at the time of
my writing, was a city founded on seven hills. But I also understood
the clue applied to both now and the future. It meant that Satan finds
solid, long-lasting geographic places (symbolized by hills) to exert
his authority (symbolized by heads) within human society. In every
generation, whether the Roman Empire or in any other time period,
Satan is at work looking for geographic places (hills) where he can
exert his authority and power.

[10]The second part of the cryptic clue: *the seven heads are also seven
kings. Five of those seven kings have already fallen, but one still exists and
is reigning. The other king—the seventh one—has not appeared yet, but
he is coming. When the seventh king appears, he will only remain only
for a short period of time.* When I deciphered this cryptic statement,
I quickly understood the immediate, present reference. Five rulers
under the Devil's influence have come, one is active in the present,
and the seventh has yet to come. But I also understood the larger truth
of the clue. It meant that Satan will work through political powers. In
every generation—whether the Roman Empire or throughout human
history—you can look back through time and see Satan's work in the
past. You can expect Satan to be working among world powers in the
present, and you should expect to see Satan working among them in
the future. He will be working in world movements, cultural powers, and political forces for a little while longer—that is, until Christ
comes again.

[11]The third part of the cryptic clue: *the sea-beast who once lived, who
does not appear to be alive now, is an eighth king.* When I deciphered
the cryptic statement, I understood there will be a pseudo-Christ-
like sea beast—a devilish force from the past that is living unseen

in the present—who will come in power as the eighth and ultimate king. His empire will seem like the ultimate society. It will appear to surpass all societies that have come before it. However, this pseudo-Christ-like beast and all the other seven kings (meaning the political powers set against God) share the same demonic devotion to Satan. As a result, they are all headed to the same eternal destruction.

¹²I also understood the symbolism of the beast's ten horns mentioned in verse 7 above. The ten horns I saw are ten future kings (referring to political powers) who have not yet received their share of Satan's kingdom in the world. When their time for ruling arrives, they will receive power to do their destructive damage for a very short period of time (symbolized by one hour).

¹³Working together in perfect unity, they (referring to the collective political forces, movements, and leaders) will give all their power and authority to serve the beast's devilish purposes. ¹⁴Together, they will wage war against the Lamb, but their war is ultimately useless. The Lamb will triumph over them because He is the Lord above all lords and King above all kings. All of the Lamb's called, chosen, and faithful followers will be standing beside Him; they will be cheering and celebrating His ultimate victory.

¹⁵The angel continued to share the symbolic meaning of what I saw and said to me, "The waters that you saw, where the demon prostitute sits, symbolically represent the multitude of people groups, nations, and languages under her influence. ¹⁶And you are really going to be surprised—astonished in fact—by what will happen next. The beast (implying false religions and ideologies set against God) and the ten horns (meaning societal and political powers) that you saw who had been working together to wage war against God, they will turn. Together, they will turn against the great prostitute! In their thirst to destroy, they will begin to hate the great demon prostitute (implying the city under her influence). They will begin attacking her and even each other. As they attack the great demon prostitute, she will be exposed vulgarly. Symbolically representing an individual set against God, her flesh will be torn apart. Symbolically representing a city and

society set against God, she will be burned down with fire. Evil will be destroying evil!

[17]"Little do the beast (representing false religions and human societies) and the ten horns (implying cultural and political powers) know, but by acting on the evil in their hearts, they are working to carry out and accomplish God's purpose! He allowed them to turn their hearts over to the beast's influence. He knew they would rebel against His authority, that they would develop an insatiable taste for inflicting pain and thirst for destruction. God knew that eventually these human societies following false religions and deceptive powers would turn on themselves and begin destroying one another. God knew they would be fulfilling His purpose and accomplishing His prophetic words foretold about Satan's ultimate destruction.

[18]"Lastly, the woman you saw (representing the Devil's influential ideology) is the great city (meaning the control center; place of primary influence) that captivates, influences, and controls the kings (referring to political and societal powers) of the earth." I understood the dual reference the angel was making. At the moment of my writing, Rome is the great city under the Devil's ideology. But in the future, there will always be a great city (or cities) where its leader and its cultural and political powers embody the Devil's ideology and spread his influence all over the earth.

CHAPTER 18

8.3 The Devil's ideology and those influenced by it will fall (18:1-3).

[1]After this angel had shown me how the demonic woman (meaning the Devil's ideology) and Babylon (symbolizing a city under the Devil's influence) would be destroyed, I saw another angel coming down from the heavenly realms. While the previous angel had focused on how the Devil's ideology, influence, and place in the world would be destroyed, this angel looked back at it after the fact. Looking back

on the final destruction, he told the sad story and fate of those who had lived under the Devil's influence.

As this angel approached, it was clear he had great authority. His radiance and splendor illuminated the entire earth.

²The angel shouted out with a mighty and powerful voice:

> "She (the Devil's ideology) is fallen! The great Babylon (the
>   world influenced by the Devil) that was admired by so
>   many has fallen!
> She has become the trash-heap, a wasteland for demons,
> A trash pile for every impure, vile, and demonic spirit,
> A trash pile of every impure, vile, and demonic bird,
> A trash pile for every impure, vile, and demonic animal.

> ³"For all nations have drunk the seductive, addictive wine of
>   her adulteries (meaning the Devil's ideologies). It led many
>   to turn away from God.
> The rulers and leaders of the earth have been seduced by her.
> Symbolically, they have committed adultery with her, which
>   literally means the Devil has captured the minds of the
>   leaders of the world, turned them away from God, and led
>   them to be unfaithful to Him.
> The economies of the world and the business people who
>   lead them have grown rich from indulging in her (the
>   Devil's) luxuries. Yet, in their financial success, they have
>   been distracted from living for God."

8.4 The Devil and all those influenced by his ideology will be judged (18:4-20).

⁴Then I heard another voice from the heavenly realms. The previous angel was looking back and lamenting the fate of those destroyed. This voice now gave a warning to people in the present—so that they could escape Babylon's judgment. The voice said to me:

"My people—God's people—get away from the great demonic
        prostitute as quickly as you can.
Make sure you are not lured into participating in her sins.
        Do not become close to her (referring to the Devil's ways
        and ideology).
Punishments and plagues are coming her way. You do not
        want to be found guilty by association, lest you receive her
        punishment and plagues too.

⁵"If we stacked up her sins and transgressions against God, they
        would be higher than the stratosphere.
And God has not forgotten her crimes against Him either.
        He has remembered every single one.

⁶"She (the city and people under the Devil's influence) will
        receive the punishment that she deserves. The same type of
        misery that she has lead others into will be given right back
        to her.
Except, in this case, God will give her double the amount of
        doom she has inflicted on others.

⁷"She has caused many to live in envious torment. She (the city
        and people under the Devil's influence) has led others into
        sad grief by dangling her luxuries in front of them.
She held them out like ever-elusive and satisfying prizes to be
        chased. But the tables will be turned. She will know what it
        is like to live in envious torment, anguish, sadness, and grief.
In her heart, she (the city and people under the Devil's
        influence) boasts that she is not a widow.
She claims she will never be sad or mourn over anything.
        She thinks she is above it all. In her mind, she thinks she is
        the queen of the universe who controls the world. She acts
        like the world is her puppet on a string.

⁸"But she (the city and people under the Devil's influence) will
        soon discover how weak and powerless she really is
        compared to God. It will only take one day for God's power

to break her boasting and totally overwhelm her. In one day,
plagues will strike her.
These judgments will bring death, mourning, and famine.
They will devastate her.
She will be utterly consumed with a burning rage of fire,
for mighty is the Lord God who judges her."

⁹The rulers and leaders of the earth who committed adultery with her
(meaning they trusted in the Devil and the world instead of God) will
weep. Those leaders who were intoxicated by the great demonic prostitute's luxuries will mourn. In utter dismay, they will see the smoke
rise from her burning destruction.

¹⁰These earthly leaders will observe her destruction from a distance.
They will be terrified by her torment. They will cry out over her:

"How horrible! How terrible it is for the great city, the mighty
city of Babylon (meaning the city and people embodying
the Devil's ideology). We put all our hopes in you as the
center of our selfish resistance and rebellion against God.
But our hopes were shattered.
It only took one hour for God to deliver His doom and
destruction on you!"

¹¹Another result of Babylon's fall (symbolizing the city and people
following the Devil's influence) will be devastating economic effects.
These business leaders and all those employed by them will weep and
grieve because their businesses will be shut down. Their businesses will
be utterly devastated. No one will buy their luxury items—¹²items of
gold, silver, precious stones, and pearls. No one will buy their designer
clothing—items made of fine linen, purple (referring to the most
expensive color), silk, and scarlet cloth (referring to the best-textured
clothing). No one will buy their costly building supplies to construct
anything—scented woods, articles made of ivory, and various things
made from costly woods, bronze, iron, and marble.

¹³No one will buy their fine grocery and home decor items—cin-
namon, spices, incense, ointments, perfumes, frankincense, wines,

olive oils, fine flours, and best breads. No one will buy their best live-stock—cattle and sheep. No one will buy their best modes of trans-portation—which, at the time of my writing, are horses and carriages. No business will be able to afford an employee, slave, or hired hand. The business owners will say:

> ¹⁴"All the ripe fruit and delicacies that you longed so much for
> are now gone. All the luxurious and high-end products you
> had your heart set on and longed for have vanished.
> All these items that distract God's people and seduce them to
> the Devil's ideology are gone; they will never be seen again."

¹⁵The business owners who sold these things—and gained all their wealth from selling them—will stand at a distance observing the great demonic prostitute's doom and destruction. They will weep and mourn over their loss ¹⁶and cry out:

> "How horrible! How terrible it is for this 'great' city. The city
> symbolized the center of the Devil's resistance and
> humanity's selfish rebellion against God.
> We lived for luxury and envied quality living. We dressed in
> the finest clothing—clothes made with fine fabric and
> beautiful colors.
> We loved our precious jewelry and the pride of glittering with
> gold, precious stones, and pearls!
>
> ¹⁷"We put all our hopes in this way of living and in our
> wealth, but it only took one hour for God to show us the
> utter worthlessness of living this way. In the snap of a finger,
> He destroyed it all and showed us how worthless this way of
> life really is!"

All the ship's captains, passengers, sailors and stewardesses, and every-one else who earns a living from their work on the sea will watch Babylon's (meaning the city and people following the Devil's ways) destruction from a distance, observing everything that is happening. ¹⁸In utter dismay, when they see the smoke rise from the great city's burning destruction, they will remain true to their disbelief, saying,

"Was there ever a city or human achievement as great as this one? There will never be a city (or human achievement) as great as this one!"

¹⁹They will go into deep grief by placing ash on their heads. I understood the symbolism because, at the time of my writing and before, deep grief is displayed by throwing dust or ashes on their heads. With great weeping and mourning, they will cry out:

> "How horrible! How terrible it is for the great city that
>   influenced the world. It symbolized the center of the Devil's
>   resistance and humanity's rebellion against God.
> We who had ships sailing the seas and were engaged in the
>   importing and exporting of goods. We became wealthy
>   through our economic trading with it. We built and
>   oriented our lives around the wealth we gained.
> Yet it only took one hour for all that to change and to see the
>   utter worthlessness of living this way. In the snap of a finger,
>   God destroyed it all and showed us how worthless this way
>   of life really is!"

8.5 The Devil and all those influenced by his ideology will be destroyed (18:20-24).

²⁰Then, the angel addressed God's people who had escaped Babylon's (the city and people under the Devil's influence) seduction and influence:

> "God's people—the people living completely for Christ—
>   you should rejoice and be exceedingly happy!
> Let the heavenly realms rejoice; let them celebrate over the great
>   demonic prostitute's demise—the Devil's demise!
> Let the apostles and prophets who carried God's message rejoice
>   and celebrate too!
> For God has judged the great demonic prostitute with the same
>   type of judgment she imposed on you! He has executed His
>   utter and complete vengeance on her (the Devil)."

[21]Then, another mighty angel approached. He wanted to show the finality of Babylon's (meaning the city and people under the Devil's influence) fate and doom. To do so, this angel picked up a huge boulder—the size of a large millstone, larger than what hundreds of men could hold—and threw it into the sea. The angel said:

> "With extreme violence, the great city of Babylon will be thrown down into destruction." I understood Babylon to symbolize the center of the Devil's resistance in the world and humanity's rebellion against God. In the present, at the time of my writing, it refers to Rome, but in the future, it could be any city under the Devil's influence.
> "Yet it all will be destroyed, never to be seen or heard from again. After the great, symbolic city has been destroyed, there will be a calm, peaceful silence.

> [22]"The faith-challenging sounds of distracting, non-God-honoring leisure—from a variety of its stringed instruments, songwriters, horned instruments, and bands—will never be heard again.
> The faith-challenging sounds of distracting, non-God-honoring industry will never be heard again. The sounds of its workers will be absent; the sound of its machinery will be gone.

> [23]"You, the people under the Devil's influence, will never again see the light of day, not even a flicker of light will you see.
> You will never again experience or hear the sounds of joyful events, not even weddings.
> You falsely esteemed successful business leaders and innovators as the world's most important people.
> You esteemed your human acts and achievements as the pinnacle of human progress, abandoned God, and led all the nations astray in the process.

> [24]"In her, the 'great' city of Babylon—which symbolized the center of the Devil's resistance and humanity's rebellion against God—was found the blood of the prophets.

> In this 'great' city, they had also seen many martyrs who had been killed for their faith. These people were never intended to experience death, but they were saved through their faith in me.
>
> But the evidence of their spilled blood demonstrated that she (meaning the Devil and his entire empire—the city and people under his influence) was guilty of a horrendous and terrible crime against God!"

CHAPTER 19

8.6 God's people will sing songs celebrating justice and victory in heaven (19:1-5).

[1]After hearing about Babylon's (symbolizing the Devil and the city and people under his influence) ultimate destruction, I heard the most powerful cheering I had ever heard. It had a character that was wholly other. Imagine a huge arena roaring from the largest event on earth, and then multiply it by infinity. That would be a small fraction of the magnificent celebration I heard.

The vast heavenly assembly making this magnificent noise was saying:

> "Hallelujah! We praise the Lord!
> Our complete salvation, all our value and worth, and our ultimate strength belong to our God.
>
> [2]"When He makes judgments and gives sentences, they are always right, just, fair, and true.
> God has judged the great demonic prostitute (referring to the Devil). He has given her the sentence she deserves for corrupting, deceiving, and leading the world to be unfaithful to its Creator.
> God has given her the vengeance she deserves for the bloodshed and the death of His servants."

³But this great assembly in the heavenly realm of God's perfection was not done celebrating. Again, they shouted in unison:

> "Hallelujah! We praise the Lord!
> The smoke arising from the burning of the demonic prostitute (the Devil) reminds us of God's goodness and His justice throughout all eternity."

⁴Then, the twenty-four leaders (representing God's people, God's Church) and the four living creatures (representing God's creation) fell face down to the ground. They worshiped God, the One who sits on the throne. Together, they cried out:

> "Yes, indeed. Hallelujah! God is more than worthy of our praise because of the great things He has done!"

⁵Then a voice from the throne spoke, saying:

> "Praise our God, all you who are His servants.
> No matter how big or small you think you are, give Him all your highest regards, thoughts, and reverence!"

8.7 God's people will sing songs for being fully united with Christ when the Devil has been eternally defeated (19:6-10).

⁶Then I heard the multitude too large to number unite in response. The sound of these united voices was so powerful. The power of their sound felt like the roar heard when standing beside the strongest waterfall or like hearing the loudest rolling thunder—multiplied by infinity.

Together, these unified voices shouted:

> "Hallelujah! Let us praise our Lord!
> Our Lord and God is Mighty and All-powerful.
> He reigns over everything.

⁷"Let us rejoice and be glad.
Let us celebrate His infinite value and worth because the time
of the heavenly wedding of the Lamb—where Christ is the
groom—has come.
The bride (meaning the Church) has been prepared for
this occasion.

⁸She has been clothed in a fine and clean, pure white linen that
was given to her"

Her clothing reminded me of how God's people are made pure and
clothed with a right standing with God through their faith in Christ.

⁹Upon hearing these praises, the angel said to me, "Write this down.
Those who are invited to the wedding supper of the Lamb—where
Christ and His Church will be forever unified—receive God's unmerited favor." And the angel continued by adding, "These are the gen-
uine declarations and assuring words of God. You can fully rely on
them."

¹⁰When I heard these words, I fell face down at the angel's feet to
honor him and give him reverence. But he stopped me before I even
got started. He said, "Do not do that! Do not revere me or give me any
of your worship! That belongs to God alone! I am just a fellow servant
alongside you—and your other brothers and sisters in Christ—who
maintains a faithful witness to Jesus. Worship God and Him alone!
For the very essence of the truth revealed by Jesus is the same truth
revealed by His Spirit that works through prophecy."

9. Even though suffering exists in the world, when Christ
comes again, He will bring an ultimate end to the
drama of human history and establish humanity's final,
eternal reality (section spanning Chapter 19:11—21:9).

9.1 Christ's victory is because of who He is, and it will bring ultimate victory to God's people (19.11-16).

[11]Everything I had just seen about Babylon's (meaning the Devil and the city and people under his influence) fall was an expanded vision of the seventh cup of God's wrath mentioned earlier [in 16:17-21], followed by a celebration of Babylon's fall. Having seen the vision of Babylon's fall, I saw a totally new vision that revealed the ultimate fate of those destroyed in the sixth cup of God's wrath mentioned earlier [in 16:14-16]. This vision gave me a glimpse into history's ultimate reality, where all human history is headed.

In this new vision, it began with seeing the coming of Christ and Him bringing every evil power under His rule. I first saw the gate to the heavenly realms of God's perfection standing wide-open. Coming through the gate, I saw a white horse approaching (which symbolized victory). The One who was riding it is called Faithful and True. The Victorious Rider (symbolizing Christ) passes pure judgments; He wages justified war on evil and sinful forces.

[12]His eyes blaze like a red-hot fire capable of burning any impurity through their judgment. On His head, He wore many crowns with each one surpassing any ever seen on earth (symbolizing that He is the ultimate Lord). The Victorious Rider has a name written on Him (referring to His virtue and character) that is of such depth and quality that finite minds cannot fully comprehend it—only God Himself can.

[13]The Victorious Rider wore a blood-dipped robe (symbolizing the holy vengeance He brought against sin and evil). His name is known throughout all reality as the Word of God. [14]The Victorious Rider leads heaven's armies as their Commander-in-Chief. The heavenly armies were right behind Him and followed Him through the gate. All the heavenly armies were riding white horses (symbolizing victory). They were clothed in fine, white, and clean linen, which represented their purity and right standing with God.

¹⁵From the Victorious Rider's mouth came a powerful, sharp sword. He wielded it against the nations and struck down any who stood against Him. The Victorious Rider fulfilled the prophetic words of Psalm 2:9 that said, "He will rule over all the people and guide them with an iron scepter." The Victorious Rider is the One who treads on the grapes in the winepress of the Almighty God's furious wrath. ¹⁶The Victorious Rider has His name written on His robe, His outer clothing (meaning His character is clearly seen by all). He also has His name written on His thighs so that, as He rides by, all can see and know for certain who He is. The name written on them is this:

KING ABOVE KINGS, LORD ABOVE ANY OTHER LORDS, AND LEADER ABOVE ANY OTHER LEADERS.

9.2 Christ's victory is certain (19:17-18).

¹⁷After seeing the Victorious Rider, I then saw an angel standing on the horizon. There was such a powerful light focused on him that he looked like the sun. With a powerful, booming voice, the angel called out to all the birds flying in the sky: "Come and gather yourselves together, for God has completed all His preparations for the great wedding supper where He will forever destroy sin, death, and the Devil and will bring His full kingdom.

¹⁸"In the wake of God's victory and destruction of evil, there will be many dead carcasses for you to feast on. Birds of the air, you will be able to eat the flesh of kings (meaning political leaders), generals and military leaders, and strong, well-respected people who did not live for God. You will be able to eat the horses, their riders, and the flesh of all people no matter who they are—business owners or employees, those highly esteemed by the world or those who are unknown—who did not live for God. You will be able to feast on all those who have stood against and not followed God."

9.3 Christ's victory brings defeat to all of His enemies (19:19-21).

[19]After seeing the angel proclaim certain coming victory, I then saw God's victory over sin, death, and a world aligned against God. I saw the beast (referring to the powers in the world influenced by the Devil), the kings of the earth (meaning the leaders and influences of the world), and all their armies gathered together to wage an ultimate and final war against the Victorious Rider on the horse (meaning Christ) and His army. They thought it would work, but the whole thing was over before it even started.

[20]The beast (referring to the devilish cultural and political powers of the world) was immediately seized and captured by the Victorious Rider's might. He also captured the false prophet [referring to the leader or leaders in 16:13]. The signs and wonders the false prophet performed, as though he were some kind of Christ-like figure, deceived many. They persuaded many people to esteem, highly value, and worship what the beast represented (which ultimately was any ideology or way of living that turned people away from God).

These deluded people's lives had been marked by the beast with his identifying mark whether they knew it or not. With the beast (meaning the devilish powers at work in the world) and the false prophet (the false religions and ideologies that support the devilish powers at work in the world) captured alive, they were then both thrown into the fiery lake that burns and blazes with the unquenchable fire of God's wrath. There, they experienced God's inescapable judgment, the one reserved for those who persist in their rebellion against God.

[21]As for all the rest—the human beings who had turned away from God and been marked by the beast—they were all killed by the sword that came from the Victorious Rider's mouth. Just as foretold, all the birds were able to eat the flesh of the fallen until they could not eat anymore.

CHAPTER 20

9.4 Christ's victory over the Devil (through His crucifixion and resurrection) begins God's reign in this world through His Church (20:1-3).

¹After seeing the doom that awaits those who stand against God, I then saw the punishment that would be given to the Devil. I saw an angel come down from the heavenly realm of God's perfection. He was holding the key to the Abyss. The Abyss represented a bottomless pit that resulted in separation from God, being cut off from the world. The angel also had a massive, great chain in his hand.

²With this great chain, the angel secured the dragon. This dragon was the ancient serpent who had enticed humanity to fall and the one who is the Devil (who is also known as Satan, and the great accuser of humankind). The angel tied the dragon (meaning the Devil) up with this chain for 1,000 years. I understood the 1,000 years symbolism. It meant that for a period of time the Devil's full power in the world would be held back by God. During this period of time, the Devil's power could not keep people from turning to God.

³Then, the angel threw the dragon into the Abyss. The angel locked and sealed it over the dragon (meaning the Devil) to keep him from deceiving the nations any more than allowed. The dragon would be locked up until the 1,000 years had ended, which meant until a time when God decided His purposes for human history were complete and that everyone had had ample opportunity to turn to Him. Once God's 1,000 years of holding back the Devil's power and His purposes for human history had been completed, the dragon (referring to the Devil) will be released for a short period of time. Doing so will allow God to decisively and ultimately finish His grand purpose for all things.

9.5 Christ's victory is experienced, in part, now by those who belong to Him (20:4-6).

⁴After seeing the devil's fate, I then saw the destiny of God's people, His Church. I saw many thrones in the heavenly realm. Those seated on these thrones had been given authority to judge and pass sentences. I also saw the souls of all the martyrs—those who had been killed and beheaded for their witnessing about Jesus and for sharing the word of God with others. The martyrs had refused to give their allegiance to the beast (meaning the Devil). They refused to worship him, his image, and any of the ideologies or movements he represented. These godly people did not have lives that were marked by the beast or were living for the Devil and his ways. These martyred servants lived and ruled with Christ during the 1,000 years (meaning during human history until a time when God decides His purposes are complete).

⁵The remainder of God's people who had died were not restored to life in a physical body until 1,000 years (which refers to all of human history) had ended. The people who had placed their trust in Christ have already experienced the first resurrection—meaning, they know of the new birth, the forgiveness of sins, and the new life that God gives to those who have faith in Him. They know the first resurrection, yet they wait for their physical bodies to be restored to life at the end of this 1,000-year period (referring to when God decides His purpose for human history has been fulfilled and Christ comes again).

⁶Holy and having a divine sense of fulfillment are all those who share in the first resurrection (referring to the new birth and new life that comes through faith in Christ). They may experience a physical death, but they will never experience the second death. Why? Because God is in control. He ultimately destroys and punishes evil. This second death experience will not touch those who have faith in Christ. Instead of receiving God's punishment (referring to the second and ultimate death), God's people will be priests. As priests, they will serve God and Christ's eternal purposes. These believers will rule in the heavenly realms with Christ until the 1,000 years (referring to human history) has ended.

9.6 Christ's victory ensures the ultimate, final, and eternal defeat of Satan (20:7-10).

⁷When the 1,000-year period (referring to the era of human history) is complete, Satan will be released from his prison. ⁸He will go out and deceive, seduce, and lead the entire world astray—whether to the North, South, East, or West. Just as God's people were invaded by Gog and Magog in Ezekiel 38, on a much larger, ultimate, and eternal scale, Satan will gather his army and lead an invasion against God's people. In number, Satan's army will be gigantic. Satan's army will have as many people as there are grains of sand on the seashore.

⁹Satan's army will march across the entire earth. They will surround God's City, the place where God's people are camped. But as they encircle God's City, fire will fall from the sky and consume and destroy Satan's entire army.

¹⁰Then the Devil—the one who had deceived, seduced, and led the people astray—will be thrown into the eternal lake of fire. This lake burns with an eternal fire of God's fury and wrath against evil. It is the same lake that the demonic beast (meaning the society set against God) and the false prophet (referring to those who led people away from God) had been thrown into. Together, in the lake of God's wrath, they will be tormented day and night, forever and ever throughout eternity.

9.7 Christ's victory ensures that an ultimate, final, and eternal judgment will come for all things (20:11-15).

¹¹After seeing the Devil defeated and cast into torment forever, I saw the most terrible thing I have ever seen—the last, final, and ultimate judgment. I saw the great, terrifying, massive white throne. I understood the imagery: the bright whiteness of the throne signified moral and spiritual purity, justice, and holiness. Everything in creation, the land below and the skies above, wanted to escape the terrifying presence of God's great white throne of judgment. But there was no place

to run and nowhere to hide. Escaping or hiding from God's judgment—His great white throne—was not possible.

¹²I saw all the dead—people considered both great and small—standing before the great white throne. The record books of all human existence containing everything that everyone had ever done were opened. Then, another book was opened—the Lamb's book of life. The Lamb's book of life identifies those who have placed their faith in Christ and belong to God.

Every individual person was judged by how they had lived their lives. God's record books had an account of everything that everyone had ever done; its accuracy on every detail was flawless.

¹³Every human being who had ever died was there, no matter what had happened to their bodies—even if they had been scattered across the sea. Death (meaning their physical bodies) and Hades (meaning the spirits of unbelieving people existing in a state of punishment) joined all the dead with their physical bodies once again. And all humans who had ever lived were judged according to what they had done and how they lived their lives. With the record books fully open and every detail of evidence brought forward, there was no room for escape—no room for excuses, debate, or defense.

¹⁴Then, the final judgment was given; the final sentence passed. Those in Hades (meaning the spirits of unbelieving people existing in a state of punishment) were joined together with Death (referring to their physical bodies), and they all were thrown into hell—the eternal lake that burns with an eternal fire of God's fury and wrath. This eternal lake of God's eternal fire is the second death—the ultimate and final death.

¹⁵If anyone's name was not recorded in the Lamb's book of life, they were hurled into the eternal lake of fire where they were burned by God's almighty fury and wrath.

CHAPTER 21

9.8 Christ's victory (after the final judgment) will bring about the creation of a new heaven and a new earth (21:1-9).

¹After seeing the final and ultimate judgment, I then saw a glimpse into eternity. I saw a new sky and a new earth. The first sky and earth had passed away. There was no longer any sea (not meaning literal seas of water but symbolically meaning there was no more evil present in the world). All creation was once again operating as the Creator intended.

²I saw God's Holy City, the New Jerusalem. I understood its meaning: God's Holy City—the New Jerusalem—symbolizes the place where God's rule is full and complete, where His people exist in perfect relationship with Him and with others. I saw God's Holy City, the New Jerusalem, descending from the heavenly realms. It was the most amazing and beautiful sight I have ever seen. The perfection of what I saw in this moment was beyond description. The only thing I can compare it to is when a pure, virgin bride—who has prepared herself her entire life to unite with only one person, her husband—is beautifully dressed and prepared for a perfect union. The pure beauty of that moment is the only description that even hints at the perfection I saw, and even that image cannot convey the amazing site of seeing God's Holy City.

³As I stood awestruck, I heard a mighty and powerful voice speak from God's throne, saying, "Look at this beautiful, amazing reality! Take it all in! The heavenly realms and the earth are no longer separated; they are united once again. God's home is now among His people. God's total existence will live and freely move among them. In God's City, all the people there will exist in perfect relationship with God, and He, in turn, will be in a perfect relationship with them and be their God.

⁴He will wipe away every tear from their eyes. Death, mourning, the need for crying, and the experience of any pain will not be there. Those things will never be experienced again by those in God's City,

for the old reality—the reality that we presently know and experience—will have passed away. A new reality of perfect union will have come.

⁵The One who is seated on the throne said, "Look! Take it all in! I am making all things new again. The work of new creation I started at Christ's resurrection has now fully come."

Then He said to me, "Be sure you write all this down, for nothing on earth has ever been more trustworthy and truer than this reality—that I am making all things new."

⁶And He continued talking to me, saying, "It is done! Everything I wanted to accomplish has been completed! I am the beginning and the end of all things. If I were a language, I would be the alphabet that forms the language. I would be the A and the Z of the alphabet and every letter in between. To those who are thirsty, I am the free, life-giving water that satisfies their needs, quenches their thirst, and never runs dry. ⁷The people who are victorious through their faith in Christ will have an eternal residence with Me in My Holy City, in My full kingdom. I will be their God; they will be My children.

⁸"But for all of those who did not turn to Me in faith—all those who were selfish, unbelievers, corrupt, murderers, sexually immoral; the ones who trust in their own abilities to achieve or produce magical things; all who value or give supreme devotion to anyone or anything other than Me; and all the liars—they will share a similar fate as the Devil. They will be thrown into the eternal lake that blazes with God's eternal fire of fury and wrath. These people will not only experience a physical death, but they will know a much worse death—a spiritual death and eternal separation from God. This death is eternally worse than any physical death."

10. The final revelation: Even though suffering will exist in this world, after Christ is victorious, it will be no more, and God will make all things new (section spanning Chapter 21:9—22:21).

10.1   The final revelation, part 1: God's new creation is a place where His people are perfectly united with Him through Christ (21:9).

⁹Up until now, I had seen seven different scenes and was about to see an eighth. The symbolism of what I was about to see next was clear—it was a reference to an eighth day of the week, the first day of a new age. When God created the earth, He worked for six days and rested on the seventh. When Christ was crucified, it was on Good Friday, the sixth day of the Jewish week. Saturday was the day of rest, the seventh day of the Jewish week. And on Sunday, the eighth day, Christ rose from the grave and inaugurated the first day of a new age and God's work of making all things new.

Up until now, I had seen seven different scenes, each with seven different sections. I had seen a total of forty-nine visions and was about to see the fiftieth. The symbolism of the fiftieth and of what I was about to see next was clear—just like every fiftieth year, in the Jewish year of Jubilee in the Old Covenant [Old Testament] Scriptures, there would be a release of every captive, the reunion of every family, and the restitution of every wrong. Having seen the seven previous visions, I was about to see an eighth and final vision, an ultimate year of Jubilee—the vision of God's new age!

In this vision of God's new age, I saw one of the seven angels who had one of the seven cups of God's wrath approach me and say, "Come with me, I want to show you the perfect bride, the wife of the Lamb." I realized the Lamb's bride symbolizes Gods people—His Church—who are perfectly united with Christ in the place where God dwells, in His Holy City.

10.2 The final revelation, part 2: God's Holy City is the perfect place for His people (21:10-21).

¹⁰And with those angel's words, I was taken to a special, spiritually enlightened place on a high mountain. It was like I had unique spiritual glasses that allowed me to see the ultimate and final spiritual reality that awaits all God's people. And as I stood in this spiritually enlightened reality, I saw the true spiritual nature of all things. The angel showed me the Holy City, the New Jerusalem (where God dwells with His people). I saw the Holy City—the New Jerusalem— fully breaking into human reality from the spiritual, heavenly realm of God's perfection.

¹¹God's glory gave the entire Holy City light. Words can hardly describe how radiant it was. Imagine the brilliance of the best jewel you have ever seen mixed with the brightest clarity from the purest crystal ever, multiply it by infinity, and then you might be one step out of an infinite number of steps toward grasping the incomparable light that God's glory gave the Holy City.

¹²The Holy City had great, high walls that could not be crossed over or penetrated. These high walls represented complete security. The Holy City's walls and gate structures were rich in meaning, and it may help to understand the City's layout.

The Holy City had twelve gates, and one of the twelve angels was stationed at each of them. On each of the twelve gates was written one of the names of the twelve tribes of Israel in the Old Covenant Scriptures.

¹³The Holy City had four walls, and on each wall were three gates. Each side of the wall—north, south, east, and west—had three names from the twelve tribes of Israel written on it.

¹⁴In addition to gates, the walls of the Holy City also had twelve foundations that secured them. On each of the twelve foundations was written one of the names of the Lamb's (Christ's) twelve apostles.

With this basic layout in mind, the significance of the Holy City's walls and gates can be seen. The Holy City—the place that is filled with God's people—was built upon God's work through both the twelve tribes of Israel (representing the Old Covenant's teaching) and the twelve apostles (representing God's New Covenant teaching).

[15]The angel who was showing me the Holy City had an authoritative, golden tape measure. He used it to account for every inch of the City, its gates, and its walls.

[16]The City was laid out in a perfect square. It was as long as it was wide. I grasped the meaning—the perfect square structure symbolized the perfection of the place where God dwells. The angel used the tape measure and found it to be 12,000 stadia (at the time of my writing, a stadia is a measurement considered to be a great distance and which has symbolic implications to the twelve tribes of Israel) in length and 12,00 stadia wide (symbolic of the twelve apostles). And then he measured its height, and it was 12,000 stadia high (a height that, at the time of my writing, is considered impossible to cross over). The City was not just a perfect square but a perfect cube! And the symbolism of the height indicates that God's Holy City perfectly unites heaven and earth.

[17]The angel measured the thickness of the wall and found it to be—in terms of human measurement: 144 cubits thick. I grasped the meaning—144 was a perfect multiple of twelve (12 times 12). The 144 cubits meant the walls comprised of the names of the twelve tribes of Israel (symbolizing the Old Covenant's teaching) and having the twelve apostles as its foundation (symbolizing God's New Covenant's teaching) were strong and could not be penetrated.

[18]Once again, words cannot accurately convey the all-surpassing, overwhelming, and incomparable beauty of the Holy City. I will try to convey the amazing nature of this sight in the best terms I can. The City walls were constructed of the most precious stones you could imagine, some type of heavenly stone that looked like jasper. The City itself was constructed of the most amazing, heavenly material that

resembled pure gold, except it was so amazingly pure that you could see straight through it like glass.

[19]The foundations of the City's walls were also decorated with a great display of precious stones made from a heavenly material. Each of the twelve foundations had its own unique heavenly decoration. I can only tell you what the earthly counterpart looked like for each of the foundations. The first foundation looked like jasper, the second sapphire, the third white agate, the fourth emerald, [20]the fifth onyx, the sixth ruby, the seventh chrysotile, the eighth beryl, the ninth topaz, the tenth turquoise, the eleventh jacinth, and the twelve amethyst. The symbolism of the twelve jewels communicated a message. Non-believers—both at the time of my writing and before—have looked to define reality through the twelve signs of the zodiac. These twelve jewels in the foundations corresponded to the jewels in the twelve signs of the zodiac. The message communicated here—the truth, meaning, and reality that non-believers look for is found in the City's walls, which are comprised of the witness of the twelve tribes Israel (symbolizing the Old Covenant's teaching) and the twelve apostles (symbolizing God's New Covenant teaching).

[21]The City's gates were made of pearls that had some sort of unique, heavenly composition. Each of the twelve gates was made of this heavenly pearl-like material. The main street that connected the entire City was also paved with the most amazing, heavenly material. It seemed like the purest gold but was so pure you could see straight through it like it was glass.

10.3   The final revelation, part 3: God will live in and among His people in His perfect and Holy City (21:22-27).

[22]The City did not have a temple. In the Scriptures of the Old Covenant [Old Testament], a temple was a building that symbolized God's presence with His people. But the Holy City did not need a temple, because the Lord God Almighty and the Lamb (referring to Christ) were actually there!

²³The Holy City did not need anything to give it light. It did not need the sun or the moon to shine on it. God's glory—which has the Lamb as its light source—filled the place with brilliant light and illuminated the entire City. ²⁴People from every nation who are in the City will walk by the radiant light of God's glory. All the rulers and leaders of the earth who are in the City will bring their God-honoring, good achievements into it.

²⁵The gates to the City shall always be open and never be shut. I got the point of these open gates, because, at the time of my writing, a city's gates would be shut to protect the people inside from various evil threats. But in the Holy City, there will be no need ever to shut or open the gates, for evil has forever been defeated, and there will be nothing to fear ever again. The Holy City and those in it will never have to fear evil lurking in the dark (symbolized by night), because it will be perpetually filled with the eternal day of God's light.

²⁶All of the best, good, valuable, worthwhile, and God-honoring achievements of human beings from every nation will be brought into the Holy City. ²⁷Nothing impure—nor anything that could defile, corrupt, or deface the eternal beauty of the City—will ever enter it. No one who could ever commit shameful, immoral, or deceitful acts will be able to enter it. Those evils and those who commit them have been eternally eradicated from God's Holy City. The only residents of God's Holy City are those whose names are in the Lamb's book of life, those who belong to God.

CHAPTER 22

10.4 The final revelation, part 4: God's Holy City in His new creation will be filled with eternal life and will have all evil eradicated from it (22:1-5).

¹Then the angel showed me how God's Holy City lived in perpetual, eternal life. There was a river containing eternal, life-giving water,

which sparkled brighter than crystal ever dreamed of being, flowing from the throne of God and the Lamb.

²It flowed through the heart of the City giving everyone in it access to eternal, life-giving water. On each side of the river—just like in the Garden of Eden in Genesis 2, before sin entered the world—everyone had access to the tree of life. Every month (which implied its perpetual, ongoing, and abundant nature), the tree of life produced twelve different types of fruit (which symbolized how the tree provided for everyone's nourishment and how no one was in need). Also, the leaves on the tree provide healing for all the people from every nation who are in the Holy City. I grasped the meaning: these healing leaves symbolize how all physical and spiritual wants will be removed from God's perfect City; all needs will be provided for and met by God.

³The effects of sin's curse on the world shall be no more; sin and its effects will not exist any longer. God's throne and rule and the Lamb of God will be in the City. All God's people will serve Him in joyous, delightful, and rewarding activity. ⁴God's people will see His face. God's character and likeness will be reflected in all His people; it will be as though God's name is written on their foreheads. ⁵There will be no more night, which symbolically represents evil. God's people will not need artificial light from a lamp or even natural light from the sun. The radiance of the Lord God will give them all the light they need. And they will rule and reign with God forever and ever throughout all eternity.

10.5   The final revelation, part 5: God's Word and final revelation need to be shared now (22:6-10).

⁶Then the angel instructed me about the reliable nature of this revelation. He said to me, "God's message and revelation to humanity is trustworthy and true. It was the Lord, through the Holy Spirit, who inspired the prophets. He sent His angel to show His servants all the things that will soon take place.

[7]"And recall what Christ said, 'Watch! Be on the lookout, for I am coming soon! Having a divine sense of satisfaction and fulfillment is the one knows and keeps the truth of the prophecy written in this little scroll-like book.'"

[8]I, John—the one writing to you—am the one God chose to see and hear these things. When I saw and heard all these things, what do you think I did? Having been completely overwhelmed by all the angel had shown me, in complete humility, I fell face down to the ground to worship the angel-messenger.

[9]But the angel said to me, "Please don't do that! It is not appropriate. I am just a fellow servant of God along with you, your fellow prophets, and of all those people who will live the teachings of this little scroll-like book. Do not worship me. Always give your worship to the only One who deserves it—God!"

[10]Then the angel told me, "Do not seal or lock up these words of prophecy and the teaching contained in this little scroll-like book. The need is too great, and the time is too near to save God's Word for later. Share it with others now.

10.6 The final revelation, part 6: God's Word, as it goes out, will reveal where people's true allegiance is and who they trust (22:11-15).

[11]"These words, as they go out, will serve as a final proclamation that will reveal where people's true allegiance toward God lies. The people who are living unjust and unholy lives will be seen as continuing in their unholiness and injustice. The ones who live immoral and sinful lives will be seen as continuing to be immoral and sinful. The people who are living justly and rightly with God will be seen as continuing to be just and right with God. The ones who live dedicated, holy lives for God will be seen as continuing to be dedicated and holy to God."

[12]Hear these words of invitation and warning from Jesus Christ:

"Be watchful! Be on the lookout, for I am coming soon to restore God's creation and God's people! I will be bringing paychecks of judgment with Me. I will give each person the exact payment of judgment he or she deserves according to what he or she has done. [13]I am the A and the Z of language and every letter of the alphabet; the first, the last, and every position in between; the beginning and the end of all things."

[14]"Having a divine sense of satisfaction and fulfillment are those who wear clothes that have been cleansed by Christ (meaning their life has been cleansed through faith in His sacrifice). They will have permission to access the tree of life. They will have a permanent, eternal pass that allows them to enter through the gates of God's Holy City. [15]However, those who do not have faith in Christ will not be let in. Those who trust in the magical achievements of their hands, continually practice sexual immorality, murder others through words and actions, serve anyone or anything other than God, and everyone who lies and deceives—they will be left outside. They will have no place in God's City."

10.7 The final revelation, part 7: God gives His final assurance to those who believe and a word of final warning to those who do not (22:16-19).

[16]"I, Jesus, have sent My angel messenger to give all of My churches this message. I am the Root (meaning the Source) and the Offspring of David (which is an Old Covenant reference meaning the promised One who would come and save God's people). I am the bright Morning Star (which is an Old Covenant reference meaning the promised One who will judge and destroy all evil)."

[17]God's Holy Spirit and the bride (meaning His people, the Church) call out, saying, "Come, Lord, and bring Your rule and kingdom!" Let every individual person who belongs to God hear this message, and they will reply, "Come, Lord, and bring Your rule and Your kingdom!" Let anyone who is thirsty for something more in life, who knows they have a deep, unfulfilled thirst in their soul—let them hear

this message. Let them hear the message's invitation—come to Christ. Let anyone who is willing to receive God's free gift of eternal, life-giving water take it by turning from his or her way of living and trusting completely in Christ.

[18]I, John, need to give one last, personal warning—a warning to everyone who hears the prophecy and teaching of this revelation. If anyone changes any of the subject matter or teachings in this little scroll-like book by adding to it, God will bring upon that person all the destruction of evil described within it.

[19]If anyone changes any of the meaning of the subject matter or teachings of this little book by taking anything out of it, God will take away that person's access to the tree of life. He will not allow them into His Holy City described in this little scroll-like book.

11. Conclusion: Christ is coming soon; be ready (22:20-21).

[20]The One who gives us these words of warning and who gave us this truthful message says, "Yes, it is true, I will be there shortly to bring My rule and My kingdom. I am coming soon."

Yes, may it be so! We await your arrival. Come once again, Lord Jesus!

[21]May the supernatural favor of the Lord Jesus Christ be with all God's people. Indeed, it is true, and true it will always be.

CPSIA information can be obtained
at www.ICGtesting.com
Printed in the USA
BVHW090221120121
597592BV00011B/182

9 780998 033310